The Strategic Finance Workout

Test and build your financial performance

DAVID PARKER

FT
PITMAN
PUBLISHING

London · Hong Kong · Johannesburg
Melbourne · Singapore · Washington DC

To Margaret, Jamie and Tom

PITMAN PUBLISHING
128 Long Acre, London WC2E 9AN
Tel: +44 (0)171 447 2000
Fax: +44 (0)171 240 5771

A Division of Pearson Professional Limited

First published in Great Britain in 1996

© Pearson Professional Limited 1996

The right of David Parker to be identified as author of this work has
been asserted by him in accordance with the Copyright,
Designs and Patents Act 1988.

ISBN 0 273 62565 9

British Library Cataloging in Publication Data
A CIP catalogue record for this book can be obtained from the British Library.

10 9 8 7 6 5 4 3 2 1

Typeset by Phoenix Photosetting, Chatham, Kent
Printed and bound in Great Britain by Bell and Bain Ltd, Glasgow

The Publishers' policy is to use paper manufactured from sustainable forests.

About the Author

David Parker, BA, MSc, FCA, is a chartered accountant who has been involved with management training and consultancy for over 25 years. He has degrees in economics and accounting and accounting and finance from Bristol University and the London School of Economics. A member of the Associate Faculty of Henley Management College, he has lectured and written about all aspects of accounting and finance to managers. For a time he lectured in the USA at the Wharton School, University of Pennsylvania, before returning to the UK. He has designed and presented courses for business managers in companies such as IBM, Sony, ICI, Shell and British Aerospace. He also presently lectures in accounting and finance on a number of MBA courses. His wide-ranging consultancy experience has been gained from his accountancy practice and his family business – supplier of laboratory equipment to schools and colleges – in which, until recently, he was managing director.

His recent publications include *The Strategic Investment Decision*, with Roger Oldcorn, published by Pitman Professional in 1996.

Contents

• • • • • • • • • •

PART TWO: IMMEDIATE ACTIONS
Financial appraisal techniques in the short term

PART THREE: LONG-TERM FITNESS
Financial appraisal techniques in the longer term

PART FOUR: THE LONG HAUL

Preface

• • • • • • • •

Is your business fit and well financially? This Workout shows you how to test and to maintain the financial fitness of your business. You will see what has to be achieved to make the business a financial success and what you have to do to keep things that way. It requires that you, the reader, carry out a lot of tasks yourself, so you can test your own financial awareness and test your understanding as you go along. You perform the workouts, the exercises and the executive actions.

I would not like to tie the strategic financial management of business in too closely with the analogy of a keep fit programme but the likeness is extremely apt. There are two reasons for this. One is that there is a very genuine sense that a business can be said to be 'financially fit'. The second reason is that financial fitness and performance can be *measured* – just as you can measure your physical fitness by taking your pulse or your blood pressure or by timing yourself over 100 or 1,500 metres. You can measure, too, the financial state of a company by listing its resources and by measuring its performance in terms of its profit or its cash flows.

The keep fit programme – The Strategic Finance Workout – has to be for the long haul. We are not interested here with losing a few pounds (of weight!) – and then putting them on again. What is needed is a programme of incremental improvement over the longer term, to maintain and possibly improve financial performance – perhaps including some fast bursts of activity from time to time. Essentially, what is required is a continuous programme which will keep the business fit – one which will keep a 'tight ship'. You may be able to run the 100 metres in ten seconds, but after that, what then? The running of a business is rather more like preparing for the marathon . . . and then running another marathon time and time again. You have to keep the business fit *all the time*. This Workout helps you do that.

In the text, there are short-term, 'aerobic' exercises and long-term, 'jogging' exercises which aim to bring the business up to scratch and then keep it in shape. In this way, the business will achieve its strategic objectives. Many chapters have a Warm-up Workout which tests your knowledge of the subject matter included in the particular chapter. There are no answers provided for the Warm-up Workouts because the questions are answered in the text. If you feel comfortable with the questions, you might wish to skate over the material in the chapter or even skip it altogether and move on to the next chapter. If you would like to know more about the issues raised by the Warm-up Workout, work through the material in the relevant chapter, taking care to complete the exercises which sharpen your understanding. All the time, try to apply the subject matter, if at all possible, to the business you are involved in or to a business with which you are familiar.

Each exercise has a suggested answer to it. It is important that you read the suggested answers because they usually form part of the flow of text. In many chapters, rather than the application exercises, you will find suggestions for 'Executive Action'. These are activities you will find useful in making sure your business keeps financially fit. You undertake these 'off-line' as it were – there are no answers to such activities, just things to do.

The book is designed for those who manage a business of their own, or who manage a business unit in a larger concern. If you do not work in a profit-making enterprise, you will still find much of the material is relevant – or you can apply the ideas presented, to a business with which you are familiar. I always feel that it is best if you can picture a particular business when applying financial techniques. In this Workout, the business can be either in the service sector or in manufacturing or distribution. The principles are the same and they can be applied to all businesses.

My sincere thanks go to all my colleagues at Henley Management College for the many discussions about the subject matter in the field of accounting and finance. The ideas from such debate have become the spark for much of the material which has gone into the writing of this

Workout. Thanks also to Richard Stagg of Pitman Publishing for the concept of the Workout and for his unswerving support in the project. Very many thanks, too, to my secretary, Geraldine Moss, who has so carefully word-processed what has been, in many cases, an almost unreadable draft manuscript. Any errors and misconceptions in the material, of course, remain entirely mine.

David R Parker
Codicote, Hertfordshire

THE FITNESS ASSESSMENT

• • • • •

Where are we now?

How to use Part One

This first part of the Workout outlines the strategic financial objectives of business.

★ Develop an understanding of the reasons that finance is so important in running a business

★ Understand how budgets are linked to strategy – and when this may lead to a need to change the strategy

★ Check on the relevance of the return on capital employed – and its constituent parts

★ Assess how profitable your business should be

★ Use ratio benchmarks to ascertain where you are now

★ Find out what to do if you find you have a planning gap

★ Develop an understanding of the 'drivers' of the return on capital employed.

How future activity is measured

The difference between strategies, planning and budgeting

....

Why financial targets are set for business

....

The relevance of financial appraisal

....

Budgetary control and business planning

....

The need to make changes in order to achieve financial strategic objectives

....

The need to achieve an adequate return on capital employed

....

The budgetary process: budgetary control

Running a business has never been thought to be easy. Not only do you have to have organizational skills to determine that what needs to be done is done when required, but you also have to assess what markets require and make judgements on such changeable things as consumers' preferences. It is also useful to be something of a seer – someone who can look into the future to forecast what the business environment will be then. It is difficult to determine exactly what is going to happen in the future, but if you are going to run a business you have to make some estimates of what is actually likely to happen. This is because business managers have to have the resources in place to meet the demands of customers – to provide the goods and services to the market when required, at prices customers are willing to pay.

Strategies, planning and budgets

From the general management perspective, strategies and plans are laid down in general terms – objectives of the business – and the finance people express them in monetary terms in financial plans and budgets. This chapter is essentially about *financial* strategy, planning and budgeting. These terms are used interchangeably in common usage but we will use them in their more limited senses throughout this Workout. First, let us define the terms in general:

★ **Strategies** are the broader, longer term plans of the business, often expressed in words rather than numbers. They may be written into mission statements or outlined by corporate management in strategic guidelines.

★ **Planning** refers to the process of setting down those strategic plans in financial terms. The reason for this is that often as not there will be alternative, or conflicting, strategies and the objective of the financial plans is to select the 'best' of the plans to proceed with.

★ **Budgeting** refers to the detailed plans required to carry out the activities set out in the planning process.

Your knowledge of the subject

Warm-up Workouts will be used in most chapters to allow you to test your own knowledge of the subject matter to be discussed. These self-diagnostic 'warm-up exercises' allow you to judge for yourself what you know of the subject. No answers are provided for the Warm-up Workouts because the questions raised are all discussed in the text.

WORKOUT

WARM-UP WORKOUT

. . . .

Do you know:

★ why are *financial* objectives – rather than any others – set for businesses?

★ what financial objectives are set for businesses – in general terms?

★ exactly what is the process of budgeting based on strategic plans?

★ what the difference is between short and long-term decisions?

Although much of the remainder of the Workout is about answering these questions, as well as others, this chapter will discuss many of the issues raised by them.

Why finance?

. . . .

When it comes to making choices between a great number of alternative strategic directions, the reports provided by accountants are very attractive in that decision-taking process. This is largely because, in financial decisions, the suggested solutions are *measured*. Financial practice is to put all the plans into a common denominator – money! This fits in well with the logic of accounting and finance, which is firmly based upon the premises of financial economics which argues that the economic objective of most businesses is to maximize profits. It is the job of finance to measure that profitability.

Accounting and finance aim to provide information to managers to help them run their business – and, in particular, to measure the profitability of their business. The processes and techniques of accounting and finance are useful to managers seeking to find their way through the minefield of corporate strategy.

Accounting and finance is about *providing information* to help with three types of decision taking – *taken at different times*.

1. **Ongoing.** The strategic review – both short and long term – which involves:
    -   Strategic decision – deciding the direction of present activity.
    -   Receiving feedback from current activity.
    -   Preparing new plans for the future.

2. **The present.** Budgetary control – involving:
    -   Budgeting. Setting out future plans in money terms.
    -   Measuring. Establishing what we have now and estimating the need for physical resources and the finance needed to acquire them in order to be able to carry out strategies in the future.
    -   Control. Reporting actual results in due course and comparing them with the original plan.

3. **The future.** Reconsidering current strategic plans – involving:
    -   Receiving feedback on present activities.
    -   Deciding whether or not to continue with present activity.
    -   Deciding when to make changes and replanning for the future.

This process is set out diagramatically in Figure 1.1.

The relevance of financial appraisal

How does a Strategic Finance Workout help in the process outlined in Figure 1.1? Does accounting provide answers to the questions of strategic choices?

No – in the sense that finance does not promote solutions. It just measures the expected results arising from the suggestions of other managers. For example, it may be marketing or R&D departments which come up with new ideas or with innovations. Accountants will not

Figure 1.1   The planning framework

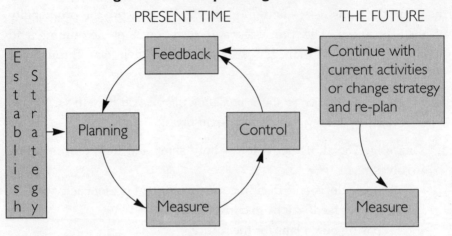

decide whether or not those ideas are to be pursued. It is for strategic management in general ultimately to make that decision.

Yes – in the sense that finance measures what resources there are and what resources are needed to carry out proposed strategies in the future. Finance states what is possible – thereby limiting the range of strategic choices that are actually feasible. In this way accounting and accountants often appear to be saying that only one course of action is really viable – and thus appearing to take the decision out of other managers' hands.

> *Finance states what is possible – thereby limiting the range of strategic choices that are actually feasible.*

The long and the short run

Finance helps us to plan for the future because it compares alternative strategies in money terms in order to select the strategies which give maximum profit. We shall see in this Workout, however, that there may be a difference between maximizing profits in the short run and maximizing profits in the longer term. This Strategic Finance Workout will help you decide which of the two routes to pursue. It may be possible to match the two strategies, but they may conflict.

The definition of a long-term as opposed to a short-term decision will depend upon the business that you are in, but for the purposes of this Workout let us decide that short term is up to five years and long term is beyond five years ahead.

EXERCISE

• • • • • • • • •

Which of the following activities would you consider short term and which long term? In each case, consider how such activities may conflict with the short or long-term plans of a business.

1 Replacing manufacturing plant and equipment.

2 Recruiting staff.

3 Downsizing and reducing the number of staff.

4 Setting up a new line of business.

5 Sales and promotion campaign for present products or services.

6 Sales campaign for a new line of business.

7 Undertaking new technology in manufacturing, or the provision of a service.

8 Providing training for staff.

9 Selecting an appropriate IT system.

10 Selling abroad.

Answer

1 Replacement of manufacturing plant and equipment would probably be regarded, for the most part, as a short-term decision – the present plant has come to the end of its life and it needs to be replaced – a pressing, short-term need. There are conflicting, long-term issues here, however. Replacement of plant assumes that things are going to continue as they have been, rather than change. This is a strategic decision in itself. Furthermore, replacement of present plant may preclude making changes required by a longer term view or at least delay such changes.

2 Items 2, 3, 5, 8, 9 and 10 may also take on the nature of short-term decisions – something done now to have expected immediate results. Each has longer term implications because each activity, albeit for immediate effect, leaves the business different from how it was before the activity was undertaken.

3 Items 4, 6 and 7 all appear to be truly longer term decisions. They will conflict with short-term decisions in that if such activity is undertaken, it may well preclude other activities.

Strategy and budgetary control

Much of what we have to say in the remainder of the Workout has to do with the process of creating strategic financial plans which aim to achieve the objectives of the business. For the time being we outline the process of budgetary control which is linked to strategic plans.

The budget is prepared with the knowledge of the past – how the company performed previously – and with managers' judgement of what is likely to happen in the future. What is done, then, is that a budget is set – usually in some detail for one year – with, perhaps, an outline for two or three years beyond that.

Figure 1.2 sets out the budgetary control and business planning process over time. Budgeting and budgetary control should be set *in the context of a corporate strategy* which is achievable over a five to ten year period.

Figure 1.2 Budgetary control and business planning

Exercise	Setting strategies	Budgetary control	Business planning	Resetting strategies
Timing	Last year	This year	Future years	Future years
Actions	Establishing strategies to achieve corporate objectives of: – maximizing value per share – profitability – growth – market share	Day-to-day monitoring of: – operations – profitability – cash flow	Forecasting 3–5 years to meet targets for: – level of sales – profit margins – return on capital – cash flow – earnings per share	Establishing strategies to achieve *new* corporate objectives of: – maximizing value per share – profitability – growth – market share

Planning and budgeting is required to set in motion activities which will achieve those plans.

Strategic objectives range from aiming to maximize value per share or profitability, to achieving specified growth in the organization or to achieving certain levels of market share for specific products or services in a market. The budgets will be used for day-to-day monitoring of performance – for control. Such control may focus on the level of operations, on profitability or on maintenance of cash flow – or on other aspects of the business, such as quality assurance or cost management. The budget will act as a benchmark against which actual results can be compared.

Current events will also affect the expectations – forecasts of future results – so there will be a continuous need to plan ahead. The reason for this is that if actual results are so far off current plans, this will impact upon the forecasts for the next three to five years. For example, if sales targets are not being met in the current period, it may be forecast that such lost business will be made up at a later date, so that sales in future periods will be higher than originally expected. Alternatively, it may be thought that the drop in current sales is likely to continue, so that the forecast for sales in all future years will be less. In either case, this has an impact upon the business resources required to service such a level of business which is different from originally expected. Changes will have to be made – and planned for!

1. *Do you have any such experience, where current activity has changed future plans?*

2. *Which resources had to be changed in such circumstances – personnel, equipment, sales channels, distribution methods?*

EXECUTIVE
ACTION

Depending upon the extent of the changes in the reforecast plans, there may be a need to reconsider the strategy. If there appears to be a permanent change in the business, there may be a need to reset the corporate strategy. The big question is whether or not the original strategic objectives can be achieved with new strategies in place. There follows two exercises on the process of budgeting and budgetary control for you to consider in relation to your business or one with which you are familiar.

EXERCISE

· · · · · · · · ·

What events in your business, or business in general, might take place which will probably lead to a need to change the strategy of the business? What actions within the business might need to be taken in the event of a change in strategic direction?

Answer

It is impossible to give a complete answer to this exercise — to list all the possible events that might cause a business to change its strategic plans — but some of the more common reasons are:

★ change in product or service technology — resulting in new products or services, rendering the old products or services obsolete

★ changes in production technology — resulting in the need for completely new equipment, possibly premises too, and rendering old factories or service centres obsolete

★ changes in consumer preferences and tastes. Changes in fashion will affect the demand for products and services, and companies supplying those markets will have to make changes

★ legislative action by governments on safety, pollution and the environment will affect the way businesses plan for the future.

The actions that management can take to change strategy are explored in some detail in this Workout but will include:

★ construction of new plants, possibly in new countries

★ major recruitment of new staff

★ major training or retraining programmes

★ involvement in R&D to improve the cost and quality of old products or services or to create new products or services

★ downsizing, reorganization or concentration on core business

★ making acquisitions or selling off parts of the business.

We are sure that you can think of many more.

EXERCISE

Given that you know the strategic context within which the budget is set, what, in your opinion, are the objectives of budgetary control?

Answer

The *principal* objectives of budgetary control are quite straightforward and may be listed as:

★ Planning for resources. An organization estimates its future activity in order to make sure that it has the necessary resources available when required to meet the requirements of the budget.

★ Co-ordinating. Making sure that all plans are consistent between departments in a business unit and with other business units within a group of companies. There is no sense in the marketing department increasing sales dramatically if recruitment has not increased the staff in the after-sales service department.

★ Communicating. The budgetary process ensures that departmental managers know what their commitment is for the year. If it is suitably communicated and managers have been suitably involved in the setting of their budget, they will 'own' their budget and will want to know how actual results have turned out.

★ Control. Actual results compared with the budget will give a degree of control – via feedback – which will (ideally) allow corrective action to be taken before things get entirely out of hand.

The activities listed in the answer above may appear simple and obvious in theory. In practice, however, they are made complex by two factors: uncertainty of the future and motivation.

1. **Uncertainty of the future.** It is exceedingly difficult to forecast future results. Rarely are budgets on target. This is not a criticism but simply a fact that what business activity is going to be in the future is just very difficult to estimate *accurately*.

   Most managers are aware of this; they live with this; and prepare budgets nevertheless to the best of their ability. They take into account all the known information and signs about the future that they can. The budget then is the best estimate of future activity in the light of current information.

2. **Motivation.** If managers are involved in the budget-setting process, it is argued that they will 'want' to know the results of actual activity compared with the budget they have been involved in setting. But which is best for motivation; to set 'tight' budgets or 'loose' budgets? The next exercise explores this question.

WORKOUT

EXERCISE

In relation to motivation and budgeting, there is debate about whether it is best to provide 'tight' budgets or 'loose' budgets. Tight budgets are achievable, but difficult to achieve. Loose budgets are easy to comply with. What advantages or disadvantages do you see (or know of from your own experience) of each type of budget?

Answer

The arguable benefit of setting tight budgets, that is those that are hard to achieve, is that managers will be pleased and well motivated if these difficult budgets are achieved. On the other hand, they may feel depressed in the more likely event of their not meeting the targets. If 'loose' targets are met, as expected, there will perhaps be no sense of achievement. Managers will not feel motivated.

Budgeting and corporate strategy

From the corporate point of view, the 'local' budgets will have to be set in the context of meeting the group's overall long-term, financial strategy. Budgets for individual business units will have to meet, in total, corporate objectives. So what are those objectives? As we have said earlier, the main financial objective of the business is to maximize profit. All the individual profit forecasts of the separate business units must therefore add to the level of profit required at corporate level.

The budget-setting process is iterative. Corporate managers will know what profit the whole group needs in order to make an overall return on capital employed. This can be compared with the total of the budgeted profits that the business units have indicated that they expect to make. Where the two figures differ, negotiations will be required to make amendments to budgets in order to achieve the overall objective. This is the essence of the budgetary process.

The return on capital employed

The maximization of profit has to be set within the constraints of that business – it is the maximum level of profit *given the particular level of resources employed*. Those resources are provided by the capital employed in the business. Thus it is usual to express profitability in terms of a *return on capital employed*. Any company, at corporate level, will know what level of profit should ideally be achieved on the capital employed and it is that return that corporate strategy aims to achieve. It is achieved, as we saw above, by setting profit targets for each business unit, which cumulatively provide the corporate profit required.

What an organization needs to achieve is a reasonable return on capital employed. This is because the providers of the capital to the business expect a return. They obtain this by way of dividends (to shareholders) or interest (to lenders). Shareholders also expect some of their return in the form of their share in the growth in the size of the business. So a

Figure 1.3   The pyramid of ratios

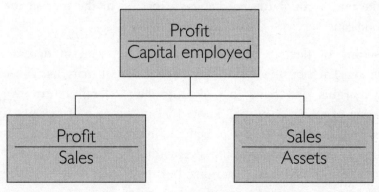

target profit figure will be based upon the desirable return on capital for the organization. In the present economic climate, the level of profit for the whole organization will have to be sufficient to provide a return on capital employed of around 10–15 per cent (as measured by operating profit before interest and taxation, divided by the total assets employed in the business).

> *What an organization needs to achieve is a reasonable return on capital employed.*

Figure 1.3 shows that the return on capital employed (profit divided by capital employed) can be broken down into two other ratios: profit divided by sales and sales divided by assets. Since capital employed equals the assets employed in the business, the following relationship holds:

Return on capital employed = Profit on sales × Sales to assets

or, in other words,

Return on capital employed = Profit margin on sales × Asset utilization

Although the overall target of, say, 15 per cent return on capital employed may be fixed, quite how a company achieves that return is not. A company may have low margins but still achieve the required rate of return by careful asset management. It is therefore difficult to set specific benchmarks or financial targets (except the overall target return to be achieved) in a particular case. The things managers can do are:

★ look at what other companies in their industry are doing (both in terms of margins and the use their competitors are making of their assets)

★ consider the marketplace and their firm's position in it

★ take into account future changes expected in the market for their goods and services.

The setting of flexible benchmarks is also relevant in decentralized companies. Each business unit may have different margins. Those with lower margins will have to make up their overall return by good utilization of assets. You may know that in the case of manufacturing, margins on sales tend to have to be high, in order to obtain the return on the large asset base. Business units providing services to customers need (and achieve!) much lower margins, but they often have relatively few assets which are required to provide the service.

Note: Remember that here we are talking of accounting assets – those included in the balance sheet. The value of employees is a major 'asset' to the business but is not taken into account in the balance sheet. Nor is the value of the goodwill of the business included in the balance sheet.

The next two exercises question the returns that managers should be seeking in their strategic plans.

EXERCISE

WORKOUT

Different business units may set themselves different benchmarks for profit margins and/or asset utilization. Do you think that each business should make the same *overall* return on capital employed?

Answer

In an ideal world, we suppose the answer is that all sectors within a group of companies should set targets which will achieve a return of the 10–15 per cent return on capital employed required by corporate strategy. In that way, by definition, an overall group, required rate of return would be achieved. But, it has to be said, there may be a number of factors which will be taken into account when setting the budgetary targets for particular business units:

★ Position in the life cycle of the business. It may be accepted that the profitability of a young business will be less than that of more mature sectors

★ State of the economy. It may be accepted that returns will not be high enough because of recession

★ Local circumstances. It may be considered that a presence in a particular market or country is important, for long-term, strategic reasons, rather than currently to be making an 'adequate' return there.

Of course, if the overall group is to make a 10–15 per cent return on capital employed and, for one reason or another, some business units are not being required to make such a return, then there will have to be some divisions within the group who are expected to make a higher return than the minimum required.

EXERCISE

Can you think of business situations which will provide higher than average returns – at least for a while?

Answer

Businesses with higher than average returns may be:

1 Businesses in the more mature market sectors, where profits are being recouped from earlier investment, the capital cost of which has been written down to zero and there is now no depreciation cost.

2 They may be businesses which are new to an industry and which are able to achieve high returns in the short run before competition arrives.

3 They may be businesses which have introduced new, cost-saving innovations in manufacturing processes, or in the provision of a service which provides a higher than average return on capital.

The budgetary process

Figure 1.4 sets out the budgetary process in a diagram. Past results are used in the preparation of the budget for the coming year. Actual results in the year are compared with budget, and variances are calculated, showing the difference between budgeted and actual results. Large variances can be investigated.

Figure 1.4 also indicates that the current year's actual results are used to forecast future out-turns:

★ Some companies forecast anew the likely results for the current year once it is underway. A forecast out-turn for the current year is thereby produced. This may then be compared with the original budget – to see how near the revised outcome for the year is to the original budget.

Figure 1.4   The budgetary process

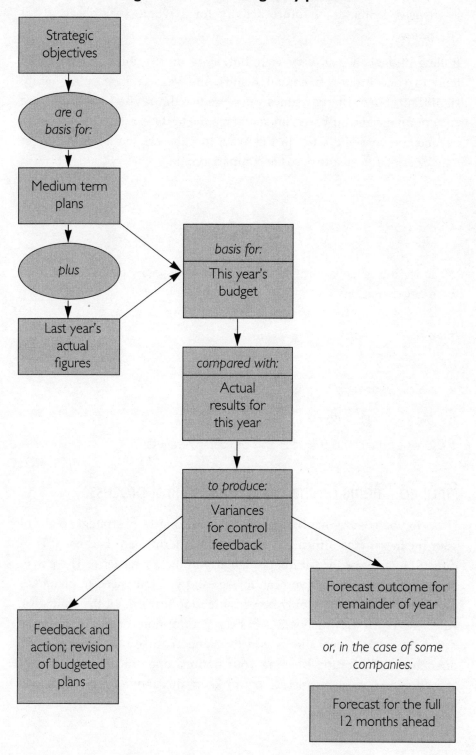

★ Other companies develop a 'rolling' budget or forecast, which revises estimates of future activity for a whole year ahead at all times.

Rolling budgets are all very well, but, since most groups of companies tend to concentrate on annual results, the year end becomes highly significant. So most companies only predict the revised results of the current financial year based on actual results to date, rather than looking beyond the year-end date. In this way, too, the original annual budget may be kept, for the purposes of comparison.

EXERCISE

WORKOUT

What are the essential strategic issues, in the budgetary process, that have to be decided upon?

Answer

They are:

★ overall budgetary targets

★ 'hard' or 'soft' budgets

★ forecast results to the year-end or rolling budgets.

Final comments on the budgetary control process

How do you ensure that budgets fit into the long-term strategic plans of your business? It is difficult to establish long-term plans because it is so difficult to forecast the future, particularly in the longer term. There may be several strategies that you can foresee and you may need to plan for a number of them. It may only be possible to follow one of the strategies. Alternatively, it may be possible to keep your options open and continue down the path which allows you to change course onto one or other direction in the future. Keeping your options open in this way is very attractive and most businesses try to keep alternative options open as long as possible.

At the end of the day, of course, it will be the successful managers that eventually opt for the right strategic decision (perhaps not closing down any opportunity for the alternatives). You will become known as a successful manager if you get the strategic investment decision right a number of times. This may lead to great economic success and recognition for the company and its strategies. Senior managers these days who make such correct strategic decisions often make arrangements for benefiting from such success by taking share options in the company in the early days of changing strategy. These share options take on great value if, at a later date, it is found that the earlier strategic decisions were in fact the right ones to take. But only time will tell.

We make the assumption in this Strategic Finance Workout that you are used to preparing budgets for the coming year or so. What we are interested in here is the evaluation of strategic plans. As we have said in this chapter, it is important that the short-term plans fit in with the longer term objectives. Really, the remainder of this Workout deals with the ways in which finance can help take the correct strategic decision in the first place.

How do we know how good we are?

Achieving the business's financial objectives

· · · · · · · · · ·

The importance of profit

· · · · · · · · · ·

How profitable do you need to be: performance benchmarking

· · · · · · · · · ·

Calculation of the return on total assets – the return on capital employed

· · · · · · · · · ·

What sort of percentage returns should you expect in your business?

· · · · · · · · · ·

How can you improve upon the return on capital employed?

WARM-UP WORKOUT

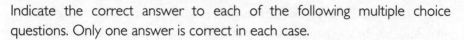

WORKOUT

Indicate the correct answer to each of the following multiple choice questions. Only one answer is correct in each case.

1 Which of the following would you say is the main financial objective of business?

(a) to ensure that shareholders receive an adequate return on their capital

(b) to grow sales as much as possible

(c) to pay staff as much as possible.

2 Which of the following would you say is the least sensible financial target to set?

(a) a specified sales volume

(b) a specified percentage profit on sales

(c) a specified level of expenditure.

3 A business needs to make a profit in order to:

(a) pay employees

(b) pay dividends to shareholders and reinvest in the business

(c) pay interest to those who have lent to the company.

4 Capital employed consists of:

(a) total assets

(b) total assets less current liabilities less cash balances

(c) shareholders' equity less reserves.

5 Asset utilization is a measure of:

(a) quality of production

(b) profitability

(c) sales generated by the use of the assets held by a business.

Business's financial objectives

Business is driven by setting an objective to achieve a certain percentage return on capital employed. This is achieved by (a) making enough profit on sales and (b) by using assets as effectively as possible. It is essential to know how good we are in each of these key areas and how this can be assessed is the content of this chapter. From the strategic point of view, the return on capital can be poor now, but it is essential that there is an expectation that the return will be adequate – and probably more than adequate – in order to 'catch up' later. Strategic financial analysis will allow time for the development of ideas, the honing of technology and the growth of markets, which will one day bring their rewards. This is quite different from a more short termist approach which will demand adequate returns now.

There is, therefore, the additional variable in budgeting: the amount of time that will be allowed for budgetary targets of return on capital to be achieved. Most companies are aware that there are some business units which will not be profitable in the near future, but that there are others that are very profitable currently. In order that the whole enterprise makes an adequate return, it is hoped that the currently profitable businesses will compensate for those that are becoming so.

Quite how this process works and how it is communicated will vary from business to business. In some companies, targets will be set in total at senior management level and then business units will be provided with targets to meet. In such cases, the local managers may or may not be offered the opportunity to refer back if they feel their targets are not achievable. In other cases, managers in business units may be empowered to achieve their own goals to the best of their ability in their own local circumstances. How does it work in your own organization? Do you feel you own the budget at the end of the planning process?

You may be given a budget for your business for the coming year. You may be required to achieve certain sales or revenue targets or you may be expected to achieve a certain level of profit for your particular operation. You may be asked to do as well as last year plus 5 per cent to allow for some growth.

EXERCISE

● ● ● ● ● ● ● ● ●

If you are someone who is responsible for running a budget, what targets are you set? What targets *might* you be set?

Answer

Targets might be based on achieving:

★ a particular level of sales revenue

★ a specified profit figure

★ a specific cash flow figure

★ a specified sales volume

★ a required return on sales (profit margin percentage)

★ spending of no more than budgeted expenditure (that is, keeping within cost limits).

Each of these have pros and cons, but most common today is the requirement to make a specified profit amount from a particular level of sales, and for some companies who wish to derive cash from their activities, the achievement of the cash flow budgeted will also be a main objective of budgetary control.

Are the following typical comments on the setting of budgets in your business? They are statements made to me recently about budgeting by business managers in two different, but very large, organizations:

'It would be better if strategies and targets (particularly cost reduction targets and marketing plans) were agreed and *communicated* to the cost centre managers to enable them to develop their individual budgets with an appropriate level of knowledge. This would assist in improving the quality and ownership of the budgets.'

'I have just received my budget (in April) for the year to December – and I have never seen any of the figures before!'

Corporate objectives

For the purposes of financial planning at *corporate* level, organizations will know the level of *profit* that they would ideally like to achieve. This is because corporate treasurers will know that in the final analysis they have to satisfy their shareholders. Shareholders expect to receive a dividend and they expect some growth in the value of their shares. The growth comes about through the extra business generated from profits 'ploughed back' into the business.

Note: It is fair to say that it would be possible to distribute all the profits to the shareholders as dividends – leaving no cash to be reinvested for growth in the business. If this were to happen, the company would grow by raising extra cash by issuing more shares. This would mean asking the shareholders for some of the cash back! This rather inefficient process is avoided by the company keeping some of the cash generated from profits to reinvest in the business annually.

The profit level required by corporate management will have to be earned by the business divisions. Ideally, the corporate planning should begin by asking business units to say what they can achieve. The view of profitability that they take for planning purposes should take into account both the short term and the longer term. Some business units may be expected to make higher than average profits – because, for example, their market is well established – whereas other businesses are growing their customer base and will not be expected to be very profitable for some years. So both the short term and the longer term need to be considered in the planning process.

> *The profit level required by corporate management will have to be earned by the business divisions.*

All the individual plans will be consolidated and co-ordinated at corporate headquarters. Senior management will know what amount of profit is required to meet the needs of shareholders. So, if the cumulative level of profit for the company as a whole that is initially forthcoming from the budgeting process of individual businesses is insufficient, it may be necessary to ask some or all business units to review their budgets – and come up with plans to make more profit – if they possibly can.

Such an iterative process takes time but, at the end of the day, it will produce budgets which will have a realistic chance of being achieved and which fit into the longer term strategy of each business unit. In this process, each business needs to be honest with itself and with its corporate managers. Each business needs to know where it is now and whether there are possibilities that it could do better. Any business can obtain some idea of whether there are opportunities to improve performance by comparative benchmarking; comparing where you are with where you would like to be or by making comparisons with others.

Performance benchmarking

The objective of financial performance benchmarking is to make comparisons of, in this case, the budgeted position with some kind of standard or benchmark. Comparisons can be made:

★ with our own past results

★ with competitors' figures

★ with targets.

Competitors' figures may be found in a number of sources:

★ trade or industry statistics

★ business databases

★ government statistics

★ libraries

★ journals

★ company published financial reports and accounts.

The return on capital employed

Any business has to make a return on the capital supplied to it by the providers of funds.

EXERCISE

• • • • • • • • •

Why does a business have to make a profit? What happens to it if it does not? Can a business afford to make an 'adequate' profit, rather than make as much profit as possible?

Answer

There are lots of points to consider in answering the above exercise. Let us take them one by one.

1 Why be profitable?

   (a) In order to give those who have provided the money to set up the business – shareholders and lenders – a return on their capital.

   (b) In order to grow. The way we account is that some of the profit is distributed by way of interest (to lenders) and dividends (to shareholders), but some is retained in the business – so the business grows. We have become so used to this feature of companies – that some profits are 'ploughed back' into the business – that we now expect growth to occur in any business

   (c) In order to be able to raise additional funds from time to time. Retained profits will not always provide enough cash for the possible growth achievable by the company. Consequently, new funds will be raised – by borrowing or by issuing more shares. It will only be possible to raise new funds if the business is profitable. No-one wants to invest in a business that is not profitable!

2 What happens if the business is not profitable?

   An unprofitable business will obviously be unable to do the things mentioned above. It will be unable to give its owners a return on their investment. It will be unable to grow and it will probably not be able to raise funds for future growth. It will therefore decline, relative to others in its industry. It may do so at such a rate that eventually it is forced to cease business altogether.

3 Can a business afford not to maximize its profits?

   There is no doubt that businesses can (and do) continue for many, many years making 'adequate' profits rather than 'maximum' profits.

Eventually, however, if a company is not making as much profit as it can, someone else will come along and do it for the company. This may mean a shake-up (shake-out probably!) of senior management. Ultimately, the company may be taken over by another company and changes will be made to improve the profitability that was inadequate. The target (the under-performing company) will probably be cheap to buy, because it is less profitable than it could be. The acquirer will improve the level of profits and gain, possibly substantially, from the takeover.

How profitable?

Having determined, in the answer to the previous exercise, that businesses need to be and are expected to be profitable, the question arises as to how profitable do you need to be. Here we need to refer again to the amount of capital in the business. What we are looking for is a *return* on the capital tied up in the business.

The return on capital employed can be defined in a number of ways. Here it will be defined as the profit before interest and taxation (the operating profit) divided by the total of fixed assets and working capital.

$$\frac{\text{Profit before interest and taxation}}{\text{Total assets}} = \frac{\text{Profit before interest and taxation}}{\text{Capital employed*}}$$

* Remember that the funds supplied by lenders and shareholders (capital employed) is put into the business in order to acquire assets for the business to work with.

In the UK currently, we would estimate that the return on capital employed measured in this way would need to be between 10 and 15 per cent. This takes into account the cost of shareholders' funds (what shareholders expect as a reasonable return), the cost of borrowing (the level of interest charged by lenders), and current levels of business risk, inflation and taxation.

Profit

• • • • •

The profit figure comes from the profit and loss account or income statement. The profit before interest and taxation is equivalent to the trading profit or profit from operations shown in a typical published set of accounts. The profit is achieved by selling goods or services at a greater value than it cost the organization to provide them – taking into account any sales and marketing, distribution and administrative costs involved. The profit before interest and taxation is as shown in Figure 2.1.

Figure 2.1   Profit before interest and taxation

	Sales	– alternative expressions for sales are revenue or turnover
less	**Cost of sales**	– the cost to the business of acquiring or producing the goods/services sold
=	**Gross margin**	
less	**Operating expenses**	– the cost of achieving the sales and running the business – including the costs of selling and marketing, distributing the product or delivering the service and the administrative cost of running the business
=	**Net margin**	– profit/earnings before interest and taxation

Figure 2.2 shows a typical profit and loss account for a UK company: Sparkle plc.

Assets

The figure for total assets will be found in the company's balance sheet. It is equivalent to all the fixed assets plus the current assets. Fixed assets

Figure 2.2 Financial accounts of Sparkle plc

Profit & Loss Account

	£000
Turnover (sales revenue)	845
Cost of sales	589
Gross profit	256
Selling, distribution and administrative expenses	198
Net profit = profit before interest and taxation	£58

include property, plant and equipment, motor vehicles and so on. Current assets are represented by stocks, debtors (receivables) and cash balances. Figure 2.3 sets out a typical balance sheet for Sparkle plc, a manufacturing company in the UK.

Figure 2.3 Balance sheet of Sparkle plc

	£000	£000
Fixed assets:		
Property, at current valuation	102	
Equipment, at cost less depreciation	130	
		232
Current assets:		
Stocks (inventory)	60	
Debtors (receivables)	157	
Cash (bank balance)	6	
		223
Total assets		£455
Current liabilities:		
Creditors (payables)		47
Long-term liabilities:		
Creditors payable after more than one year		68
Shareholders' equity:		
Share capital	120	
Reserves	220	
		340
		£455

EXERCISE

· · · · · · · · ·

The return on capital employed for the company which is shown in Figures 2.2 and 2.3 amounts to 12.7 per cent. Can you calculate this?

Answer

The return on capital employed of Sparkle plc is:

$$\frac{\text{Profit before interest and taxation}}{\text{Total assets}} = \frac{£58,000}{£455,00} = 12.7\%$$

The elements of the return on capital employed
· ·

The return on capital employed of 12.7 per cent for Sparkle plc is a good return. It might be possible to improve the return by careful planning. Further analysis and comparative studies might indicate where improvements could be made in order to make a better return over another year. The best way of seeking how the rate of return on capital employed might be improved is to break the ratio down into two subsections:

★ profit margin on sales, and

★ asset utilization.

Figure 2.4 indicates the inter-relationship between these two ratios and the return on capital employed. Basically, the profit margin ratio multiplied by the asset utilization figure will give you the return on capital employed The 'pyramid of ratios', as it is called, shown in Figure 2.4 is a very useful way of exploring further the actual return on capital employed which is currently achieved.

Figure 2.4　Pyramid of ratios

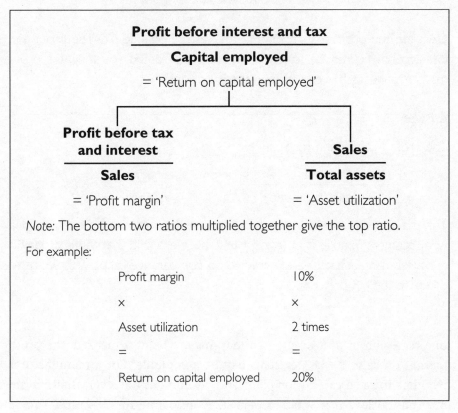

$$\frac{\text{Profit before interest and tax}}{\text{Capital employed}}$$

= 'Return on capital employed'

$$\frac{\text{Profit before tax and interest}}{\text{Sales}}$$

= 'Profit margin'

$$\frac{\text{Sales}}{\text{Total assets}}$$

= 'Asset utilization'

Note: The bottom two ratios multiplied together give the top ratio.

For example:

Profit margin	10%
×	×
Asset utilization	2 times
=	=
Return on capital employed	20%

Profit margin on sales

The profit margin on sales ratio indicates the average return achieved on sales. The margin percentage depends on the business:

★ labour intensive businesses or those that are in very competitive markets or those with high volume (and fast moving stocks, if they have them) tend to have low profit margins, sometimes as low as 3 or 5 per cent.

★ capital intensive industries or those at the quality end of the market will have much higher margins – in the range of 10–15 per cent.

In order to calculate the profit margin on sales, simply divide the profit on ordinary activities before interest payable and taxation by the turnover – both found in the profit and loss account.

EXERCISE

· · · · · · · · ·

Calculate the profit margin ratio in the case of Sparkle plc. The profit and loss account figures are to be found in Figure 2.2. Do you think the profit margin Sparkle achieves is a good margin or not?

Answer

The profit margin ratio for Sparkle is:

$$\frac{\text{Profit before interest and taxation}}{\text{Sales turnover}} = \frac{£58m}{£845m} = 6.8\%$$

This may or may not be a good margin on sales, because we have no idea what business Sparkle is in (except that we were told that the company is a 'typical manufacturer') and we have no comparative ratios with which to compare the 6.8 per cent.

In a recession or at a time when margins are being squeezed, the profit margin on sales of 6.8 per cent may be acceptable. For a manufacturer who has to raise capital for plant and equipment however, that margin may be too low if it were to persist. A guideline for this ratio – for a manufacturer and in an ideal world – would be around 10 per cent.

Asset utilization

This shows how well a firm uses its assets. The ratio depends on the type of business: manufacturers tend to have more assets but would probably try to achieve a ratio of at least 2.0 times; retail stores, at the other end of the scale, tend to have higher ratios than manufacturers because they are less capital intensive. The ratio may not be very meaningful for service sector businesses, some of whom require few fixed assets for their activities.

The asset turnover calculation for our manufacturing company is calculated by taking the turnover figure and dividing by the total assets:

$$\frac{\text{Sales turnover}}{\text{Total assets}} = \frac{£845m}{£455m} = 1.86 \text{ times}$$

EXERCISE

• • • • • • • • •

Complete the blank boxes in Figure 2.5.

Figure 2.5 Calculating the return on capital employed

	Return on capital employed		Profit margin		Asset utilization
		=		×	
A	15	=		×	3.1
B	25	=	2.0	×	
C		=	9.0	×	2.0
D	20	=		×	3.4

Answer

A	Profit margin	=	4.8%
B	Asset utilization	=	12.5 times
C	Return on capital	=	18.0%
D	Profit margin	=	5.9%

The return on capital calculations in the exercise above show very different profit margin percentages and asset utilization figures. For example, the 15 per cent return on capital employed in ratio A is achieved with a fairly low profit margin but with a high level of asset utilization. Ratio C indicates a high profit margin but only an average asset utilization. They may well be *representative* of different sectors of industry. The next exercise asks you to consider which industry each of the four groups of ratios used in the previous exercise might represent.

WORKOUT

EXERCISE

Which of the types of business listed below do you consider most closely identify with the four groups of ratios in the last exercise? Put the appropriate letter in the boxes below associated with ratios A, B, C or D from the previous exercise.

a manufacturer (a computer mother board assembler) ☐

a distribution and wholesale business (a stationery supplier) ☐

a retail business (a supermarket) ☐

a service business (financial software producer) ☐

Answer

Type of business	Ratio group	Reason
Manufacturer	C	Relatively high profit margin times average use of assets.
Distributor	A	Relatively low profit margin but good use of assets.
Retailer	D	Relatively low profit margin but good use of assets.
Software producer	B	Low profit margin but high utilization of relatively few assets compared with sales.

The dynamics of financial ratio analysis

The groups of ratios used in the last two exercises are not necessarily true ratios for the particular business sector, but they are 'typical' in a very general sense for any one company in any one year. As investment will, in principle, be attracted to sectors with the highest returns (subject to risk considerations) all investment will be directed to the businesses represented by ratio B above! This higher return is unlikely to continue in the longer term. More and more investors will see the higher returns and they will finance other producers or providers of the service to enter the market. Such competition will drive down profits until the return on capital is 'normal' once more.

Reviewing the current year – benchmarking

If we take Sparkle plc's primary ratios calculated earlier and compare them with industry average figures as in Figure 2.6, we have a better insight into our manufacturing company. The profit margin on sales is a little below average; the asset utilization is also a little below average. This is a good indication that Sparkle should look into the reasons why its margins are lower and its use of assets slightly worse than the industry average. There is, of course, a problem with making these comparisons without a lot more knowledge of the actual business and much more awareness of the assets it needs to operate. It is very difficult to draw any conclusions about the

Figure 2.6   Comparative figures for Sparkle plc

	Sparkle's ratios	Industry average ratios
Return on capital employed	12.7%	14.2%
Profit margin on sales	6.8%	7.5%
Assets utilization	1.86 times	1.9 times

company's performance. We cannot be certain that Sparkle is worse than average; but we can say that if this situation were to persist in the longer run, Sparkle would find it difficult to attract capital should the company ever need it for expansion or other development plans. From a strategic audit point of view, Sparkle's managers will know that they have to improve their performance – or have very good reasons why they do not perform to the industry average.

There are alternatives to making comparisons with industry average figures:

★ it might be better – for benchmarking – to compare Sparkle's statistics with the *best in class*, that is with the company in the industry which has the highest return on capital employed

★ it might be better to make comparisons with the *past results* of the company – to see whether there is improvement

★ it might be better to make comparisons with some *ideal* benchmark figures or some budgetary *target*.

The next exercise asks you to calculate benchmark ratios for Sparkle from last year's financial figures and to draw some conclusions about this year's results.

WORKOUT

EXERCISE

・・・・・・・・

1 Using the previous year's accounts of Sparkle plc set out in Figure 2.7, calculate the primary ratios for Sparkle for that year. That is, compute:

– the return on capital employed
– the profit margin on sales
– the asset turnover ratio.

2 Can you draw any conclusions about the performance of the current year, now we know how well the company performed last year?

3 If the results for this year, shown in Figures 2.2 and 2.3 in this chapter, were the result of the *budgetary* process for this year – rather than the actual figures, so that changes could be made – what suggestions would you put forward in order to improve the budget?

Figure 2.7 Previous year's accounts for Sparkle plc

Profit and loss account		£000
Turnover (sales revenue)		809
Cost of sales		550
Gross profit		259
Selling, distribution and administrative expenses		191
Net profit = profit before interest and taxation		68

Balance sheet

Fixed assets:		
Property, at current valuation	91	
Equipment, at cost less depreciation	110	
		201
Current assets:		
Stocks (inventory)	55	
Debtors (receivables)	129	
Cash (bank balance)	17	
		201
Total assets		402
Current liabilities:		
Creditors (payables)		34
Long-term liabilities:		
Creditors payable after more than one year		56
Shareholders' equity:		
Share capital	120	
Reserves	192	
		312
		402

Answer

1 Calculations of the primary ratios. This year's figures are in brackets.

$$\text{Return on capital employed} = \frac{68}{402} = 16.9\% \quad (12.7\%)$$

$$\text{Profit margin on sales} = \frac{68}{809} = 8.4\% \quad (6.8\%)$$

$$\text{Asset utilization} = \frac{809}{402} = 2.0 \text{ times} \quad (1.86 \text{ times})$$

2 You can see that the year before the return on capital employed was 16.9 per cent. This was made up of a profit margin of 8.4 per cent multiplied by an asset utilization of 2.0 times. The results this year, by comparison, are all lower. The return on capital is some 4 per cent less; the profit margin has fallen by about 1 per cent and asset utilization has fallen to 1.86 times from 2.0 times.

Note: On the face of it, only small changes in the ratios have taken place, but in finance such small differences matter. Just think how pleased you are to receive a 1 or 2 per cent increase in your salary. Very small changes in profit margins or in asset utilization usually have quite dramatic effects on the return on capital employed. A decrease in profit margin of 'only' 1 per cent and a fall of asset utilization from 2.0 to 1.86 times, as in this case, has a detrimental effect of 4 per cent on the return on capital employed. There is a considerable difference between a return of 16.9 per cent and only 12.7 per cent.

3 If this year's ratios were the result of budgetary figures for the year, they would indicate that Sparkle expect margins to be squeezed this year. They are expecting an increase in sales of between 4 and 5 per cent, so the asset utilization figure should not be lower. They would need to review the planned asset balances to see where more assets are being employed this year compared with last.

The lower overall return on capital employed may upset the shareholders in due course. They may have experienced the higher return of last year for a number of years and will be unhappy when faced with a lower return – if that is the actual result of this year's activities.

The question would be: can the corporate managers of Sparkle do anything about the falling returns? If the current year's figures are the final budget for the year, presumably not much can be done about this year's figures – they are the best that can be expected. What the shareholders will need to know eventually is that steps are being taken to recover the situation. Management will need to convince the shareholders that the action being taken will result in improving the return on capital employed in the longer run.

Further analysis

So far we have used very few ratios in our exploration of our manufacturing company's return on capital employed. Even using the limited information to be found in Sparkle's accounts, much more analysis could be carried out. For example, we could:

★ find out whether the lower sales margin was due to the gross profit margin having decreased

★ find out whether selling, distribution and administrative expenses were relatively higher one year as compared with the other

★ find out whether the (marginally) lower asset utilization ratio was the result of employing specifically more *fixed* assets in relation to sales in one year compared with another

★ find out whether the control of working capital was more or less efficient – looking at inventory and receivables values in particular.

Figure 2.8 shows the calculations for the current year's figures for Sparkle plc covering the suggestions listed above.

Figure 2.8   Further analysis ratios

Gross profit margin:

$$\frac{\text{Gross profit}}{\text{Sales}} = \frac{256}{845} = 30.3\%$$

Selling, distribution and administration expenses in relation to sales:

$$\frac{\text{Expenses}}{\text{Sales}} = \frac{198}{845} = 23.4\%$$

Fixed asset utilization:

$$\frac{\text{Sales}}{\text{Fixed assets}} = \frac{845}{232} = 3.6 \text{ times}$$

Stock days (see Note):

$$\frac{\text{Stock}}{\text{Cost of sales}} \times 365 = \frac{60}{589} \times 365 = 37.2 \text{ days}$$

Debtors days:

$$\frac{\text{Debtors}}{\text{Sales}} \times 365 = \frac{157}{845} \times 365 = 67.8 \text{ days}$$

Note: It is conventional to indicate *current* assets' utilization in terms of 'days' of stocks and debtors held; thus the ratio is multiplied by 365 (= number of days in the year). The stock days' ratio is calculated using *cost* of sales because stock is stated at its cost in the balance sheet.

EXERCISE

● ● ● ● ● ● ● ● ●

Using the guidance boxes in Figure 2.9, calculate the ratios for last year. Compare your answers with the ratios shown in Figure 2.8, based on this year's results. What information does this comparison provide?

Figure 2.9 Further analysis ratios for last year

Gross profit margin:	$\dfrac{\text{Gross profit}}{\text{Sales}}$ =	─── =	☐
Selling, distribution and admin:	$\dfrac{\text{Expenses}}{\text{Sales}}$ =	─── =	☐
Fixed asset utilization:	$\dfrac{\text{Sales}}{\text{Fixed assets}}$ =	─── =	☐
Stock days:	$\dfrac{\text{Stock} \times 365}{\text{Cost of sales}}$ =	─── =	☐
Debtors' days:	$\dfrac{\text{Debtors} \times 365}{\text{Sales}}$ =	─── =	☐

Answer

Gross profit margin:	$\dfrac{\text{Gross profit}}{\text{Sales}}$ =	$\dfrac{259}{809}$ =	32.0%
Selling, distribution and admin:	$\dfrac{\text{Expenses}}{\text{Sales}}$ =	$\dfrac{191}{809}$ =	23.6%
Fixed asset utilization:	$\dfrac{\text{Sales}}{\text{Fixed assets}}$ =	$\dfrac{809}{201}$ =	4.0 times
Stock days:	$\dfrac{\text{Stock} \times 365}{\text{Cost of sales}}$ =	$\dfrac{55 \times 365}{550}$ =	36.5 days
Debtors' days:	$\dfrac{\text{Debtors} \times 365}{\text{Sales}}$ =	$\dfrac{129 \times 365}{809}$ =	58.2 days

WORKOUT

Using the data you have calculated in Figure 2.9, we can compare this year's budgeted figures with last year's figures as follows:

	This year	Last year
Gross profit margin	30.3%	32.0%
Expenses compared with sales	23.4%	23.6%
Fixed asset utilization	3.6 times	4.0 times
Stock days	37.2 days	36.5 days
Debtors' days	67.8 days	58.2 days

Armed with this additional information we can see that Sparkle, in almost every sense, is performing worse than last year (or is expected to perform worse, if this year's figures are this year's budget). There may be good reasons for the deterioration in performance. Provided Sparkle's management are aware of the situation they will be able to 'manage' it. There is some indication that they are aware of it – the expenses/sales ratio has improved, suggesting already a tightening of belts!

Take care using ratios

In this chapter, we have seen that with a very few ratios, suitably benchmarked against another company or against the company's own previous performance, you can obtain a very clear idea of 'where the company is now'. You can establish what areas of performance are good and which are not so good. But clearly, the ratios set up questions for managers to attend to. Ratio analysis raises the questions – it does not provide the answers.

Ratio analysis raises the questions – it does not provide the answers. In fact, it is dangerous to make too many assumptions from ratio analysis.

In fact, it is dangerous to make too many assumptions from ratio analysis. Usually, you are only looking at one or two years of the history of the company. For sound strategic financial management, you need to look much further ahead. It was suggested earlier that for strategic planning purposes, the business should look five to ten years ahead.

None the less, ratio analysis will provide an insight into the current financial status of the company, quite readily, without too much effort. It is up to management to make sure that they get their message across to potential investors as to just exactly what they are to achieve in the future – to keep the good things as they are and to improve on the poorer results.

Recognition of the planning gap

What happens if the return on capital expected is not enough

············

What needs to be done if there is a planning gap

············

The drivers of the return on capital

············

The impact of making changes in the drivers

············

The effect of short-term as opposed to long-term actions

············

Growth versus downsizing

············

Strategic planning

WARM-UP WORKOUT

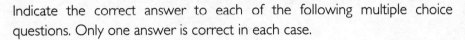

Indicate the correct answer to each of the following multiple choice questions. Only one answer is correct in each case.

1 The planning gap arises because:

    (a) there is a difference between what is expected will be achieved and what is required to be achieved

    (b) there is a difference between what can be achieved and what is required to be achieved

    (c) there is a difference between expectations and achievements.

2 Which one of the following do not 'drive' the return on capital employed:

    (a) volume of goods or services sold

    (b) amount of funds employed in the business

    (c) the level of fixed assets used in the business.

3 When reviewing the sales price driver which one of the following is relevant:

    (a) an awareness of the price of near substitutes

    (b) an awareness of core competencies

    (c) an awareness of the plant or equipment used in making the product or in providing the service.

4 The difference between strategic planning and short-term planning is that:

    (a) short-term plans relate to the immediate future and have no effect on the future

    (b) short-term plans are undertaken in the short term but might very well have long-term effects

    (c) strategic plans can only be undertaken in the longer run.

5 The main source of funds for strategic growth comes from:

(a) new shares issued to shareholders

(b) funds borrowed from banks or other lending institutions

(c) profits ploughed back into the business.

Return on capital

The objective of business is to achieve a reasonable rate of return on capital employed. Shareholders require a return on their investment. If they do not receive it – or expect to receive it – they will take their money elsewhere. So, if the return is inadequate, action will have to be taken sooner or later. How immediate the action needs to be will depend upon how urgent the investors feel the remedial action should be. Or, to put it another way, how long management can persuade investors to wait for results. It is conceivable that the current lower return on capital is because the business is building for the future – and will promise high returns then! But can the company persuade the capital markets that there will be 'jam' tomorrow?

> *Shareholders require a return on their investment. If they do not receive it – or expect to receive it – they will take their money elsewhere.*

The kind of analysis which was carried out in the last chapter, would give any business some idea how it compared with its competitors, or at least with its own results of previous years. Such analysis might indicate that something needs to be done, as it gives an indication as to 'where we are now', but compared with some particular benchmark. Such analysis does not give any indication as to what ought to be done. Certainly, each individual business unit would need to be analysed to see whether the problems were company-wide or only in individual areas of the business's activity.

EXERCISE

· · · · · · · · ·

Why do we need to look closely at individual business units, rather than at the business as a whole?

Answer

Most firms will consist of a number of businesses:

★ some of which will be doing well, clearly growing and perhaps with higher than average return on capital

★ others will be maintaining their position in the market but not making more than an average rate of return on capital

★ some may be growing but presently do not make even a satisfactory return. It is these businesses that might need protecting and nurturing if it is thought that *strategically* they are the future of the company as a whole

★ finally, there will be some businesses that have a poor return currently and where there is no expectation of growth. A question mark will fall upon these businesses. If they are giving an inadequate return, should they be continued?

What needs to be done – the planning gap

· ·

The comparative analysis of business units may indicate that changes need to be made. The appreciation that changes have to be made comes from the realization that plans do not appear to be meeting the required objectives of the business. There is a 'planning gap'. This gap between a company's desired position and where it expects to be will mean that budgets will have to be reviewed – worked through again – to see where improvements in plans can be made so that the objectives of the company are achieved – or, at least, as nearly achieved as is possible in the circumstances.

Figure 3.1 suggests what might happen if a planning gap is perceived. A is the required rate of return, but current plans indicate that only C

Figure 3.1 The planning gap

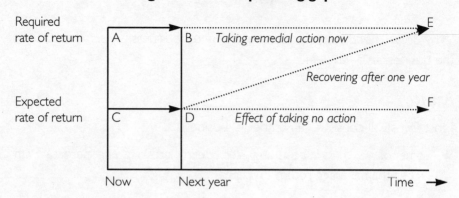

will be achieved. There are any number of possible plans of campaign in this situation. Let us consider just three.

1. Take immediate action upon the plans so that they are amended now and the rate of return indicated by AB is achieved next year. Future years also achieve the required rate of return, along the line BE.

2. Current plans are left to run their course over the next year. It is far from certain that the lower expected rate of return will actually be achieved. The actual return may be better than expected (or worse!) During next year, if only the return CD is actually achieved, plans may be put into place to improve the rate of return – perhaps over a number of years – along the line DE.

3. No action is taken and the lower expected rate of return continues to be made next year and in future years, along the line DF.

We have said that the objective of the business – from the financial point of view – is to achieve the maximum return on capital employed. If the current plans do not seem to be achieving this, managers will have to look again at the plans that have been drawn up. It may be necessary to make changes to the plans in both the short term and the long term. We investigate later in this chapter the impact that short-term amendments to plans might have on the long-term success of the business. For the time being, we turn to looking at how we might review the constituents of the return on capital employed, in order to suggest what changes might be made to improve upon a planned return on capital.

The drivers of return on capital employed

When we look at the factors that go into making the return on capital employed in more detail, we find that there are a number of 'drivers' of financial return. The importance of this is that each driver can be acted upon; they can be 'driven' so the business succeeds. Each driver can be reviewed in the context of strategic planning too; new forecasts can be made about it and strategic views can be taken about it. Taking the objective of business to be to achieve maximum return on capital employed, Figure 3.2 shows how the make-up of the return on capital employed can be described in terms of six drivers.

The calculation of the return on capital employed can be broken down into six key elements as shown in Figure 3.2. Each of them can be controlled or managed – and decisions have to be taken for each of them. This approach suggests that we can 'drive' the business from the financial point of view, if we concentrate attention on the six factors of return listed in Figure 3.2.

Figure 3.2   Drivers of return on capital employed

Return on capital employed		Drivers of return on capital employed
	1	Sales price(s) *multiplied by*
	2	Sales volume *equals*
		Sales turnover *less*
	3	Cost of sales *less*
Net profit	4	Expenses
divided by		*divided by*
Capital employed	5	Fixed assets *plus*
	6	Working capital

In very simple terms, the following action on each driver will probably be considered:

1. **Sales price.** Increase prices to improve profit. (We will see later that it is difficult to *reduce prices* and *improve profits* – even though you probably sell more – see the exercise below.)

2. **Sales volume.** Increase volume to increase revenue and thereby profit.

3. **Cost of sales.** Reduce cost of sales by careful management of materials, labour production costs and overheads.

4. **Expenses.** Reduce expenses relating to the running of the business.

5. **Fixed assets.** Check on the utilization of fixed assets to make sure that they are all essential to the business.

6. **Working capital.** Control working capital in order to minimize the capital tied up in current assets.

EXERCISE

WORKOUT

Can you envisage a number of alternative situations from those listed above, where *contrary* activity might be employed to improve the return on capital employed? For example, managers might argue that profit could be improved if prices were *reduced* or if expenses were *increased*.

Answer

1 Sales price decreases. It might be that volume will increase substantially enough to make higher profits at lower prices. It is unlikely that this will be so because of the behaviour of costs, which we explain in Chapter 4. It is possible to increase profit by taking on *extra* business at lower prices, and this situation is also explained in Chapter 4.

2 Sales volume. We cannot think how lower volume can lead to greater profit. It may be so in the longer term if lower volumes mean improved quality of product or service which, in turn, eventually leads to increased sales and higher profits.

3 Cost of sales improvements. Most organizations these days constantly review the elements of cost which go to make up the cost of supplying the product or service to the market. Production cost control techniques have been a feature of businesses for the last 100 years. Great innovations have been made, particularly in creating cost effective production lines. In the last 20–30 years, attention has been focused also on the cost and effectiveness of providing services. Computer and communications technology have brought about vast changes in the way services are now delivered to customers.

4 Increasing the amount spent on selling, marketing, distribution and administration. It is quite conceivable that revenue can be increased by spending more on, for example, sales and marketing. A sales campaign is likely to increase revenues but whether the resulting increase in gross profit will be enough to have made the sales campaign worthwhile, is, of course, the marketing manager's dilemma.

We are quite sure you can think of other examples, where more expenditure leads to more sales. For example:

   – increased spending on training might improve efficiency of a business that customers like to do business with

   – increased technical training may result in engineers and others developing new products or services which will increase sales and profits

   – increased spending on distribution methods may cause products or services to get to customers more efficiently so that more sales are generated.

5 Increasing expenditure on fixed assets. Acquiring new, up-to-date equipment may well result in productivity improvements which outweigh the cost of the new fixed assets. We look further at the use made of fixed assets in Chapter 5.

6 Increasing the amount of working capital. It is possible that companies with high levels of stocks of goods for resale will be able to make sales because they have the items in stock. Other companies with slimmer stock levels might miss out. However, as we shall show in Chapter 6, having too much working capital is a great burden for the business to carry.

The effect of short and long-term actions

When we investigate the underlying drivers of the return on capital employed, we have to remember that we are living in a dynamic environment. Some business environments these days are changing very rapidly indeed. This often makes it very difficult to stand back, take the long-term view and to see what action it is best for the firm to take for the longer-term interests of the business. Managers often just do not have the time. They are so busy mopping up the problems created by the change they see all about them! The action they take *tends* to be short term.

Can you think of any examples, in your own experience, which appear to be knee-jerk reactions to a current situation? Did any of your examples of short-term actions taken have long-term ramifications for the business?

Seeing a 'planning gap' leads to a review of the drivers

The review of any of the return on capital employed drivers may suggest that action be undertaken to take urgent effect in the short term, but in an ideal world the long-term effects of current actions should also be considered. The reason for this is that there may well be conflicting results from short-term actions on the one hand and long-term actions on the other. Three examples are:

1. A sales promotion campaign may increase sales initially but sales may tail off later if the level of promotional activity declines. Ideally, it should leave a lasting impression on customers or clients so that they continue to think of the specific product or service when they buy again.

2. Cost savings which may make for higher profits in the short term but where sales decline in the longer term because quality has fallen.

3. Staff headcounts which are controlled to contain costs in the short term but where morale falls in the longer term with consequent lower output and efficiency then.

Study and consideration of the drivers may lead to activities which will improve returns quickly. These might be called 'short-term remedies'. Alternatively, it might lead to activity which will effectively change the nature of the business in the longer term. These activities are usually regarded as those which are 'strategic activities'. It is not an important issue, but most managers would regard a strategic decision as one which considers the fundamentals of the business – and these can usually only be effected in the longer term. Short-term activities are thought not to have any strategic relevance, but as we have suggested above, short-term actions may well affect long-term strategy. This is because the short-term activity, in some cases, may well make it impossible to undertake certain long-term plans.

If we consider the way in which the drivers of return on capital might be considered in the longer term we can draw the following list of strategic questions that need to be asked in any business.

1. In relation to the sales price driver:
    –   an awareness of competition and competitors' prices
    –   an awareness of product differentiation
    –   an awareness of the prices of substitutes.

2. In relation to the sales volume driver:
    –   an awareness of markets
    –   an awareness of where growth might come from
    –   an awareness of where developments might come from.

3. In relation to the cost of sales driver:
    –   an awareness of core competencies
    –   an awareness of the cost base
    –   an awareness of developments in the techniques of producing the product or of providing the service.

4. In relation to the expenses driver:
    –   an awareness of resources and what can be achieved with them
    –   an awareness of technological changes coming along which will save costs.

5. In relation to the fixed assets driver:

    –   an awareness of resources and what can be achieved with them

    –   an awareness of technological changes coming along which will save costs.

6. In relation to the working capital driver:

    –   an awareness of stock control and credit control procedures that will keep the amount of working capital under control.

Growth

· · · · · · · ·

The importance of growth to a business was explained in Chapter 2. It is a truism that businesses cannot stand still. They either grow or decline. In a changing world it is likely that the rate of growth or decline will be rapid. For one reason or another the size of the market for a firm's goods or services will grow or decline, the nature of products and services will change and new ideas and innovations will enter the scene to alter the level of business for anyone found within an industry.

EXERCISE

· · · · · · · ·

WORKOUT

Can you remember the other reason why a business will grow rather than remain more or less the same size? [Hint: Do you remember the dynamics of the accounting process that was described in Chapter 2?]

Answer

Businesses have to grow in order to satisfy the shareholders. The accounting dynamics of the situation are that the shareholder receives a return by way of a dividend – which is part of the profits of the company. They also receive part of their return from the growth in share price. This occurs because some of the profits are ploughed back into the business – which increases the size of the business and thus the share price grows.

Downsizing

It is possible for a company to decline in size and yet to survive. There have been many examples of this in the recession of the 1990s. Activities such as downsizing, rationalization and business process re-engineering are techniques which have been associated with reducing the size of the business, or at least doing more with the same resources. Usually, the attack is upon the cost base of the company, but that inevitably means a lower level of sales subsequently. Companies that have undertaken major reorganization of this kind have diminished in size. IBM is an example of a company that had to downsize. Such action often leads to a fall in the share price.

Subsequently, perhaps ironically, cash is generated from the profits of the reorganized company. But in the short term, immediately after re-organization, there is no need for the cash to be ploughed back into the business, since there is no expectation of growth then. Very often such companies have simply used the cash generated from downsizing to repurchase their own company's shares on the stock market. By buying back its own shares which are often at a low value, the company is able – with its own cash – to support the share price by increasing the demand for shares. IBM did exactly that. They acquired 10 per cent of the company's own shares in 1995.

Strategic planning

Having recognized that something is to be done, the following steps have to be taken in order to assess what action needs to be taken in the future.

★ Find out where we are now. What resources do we have? What resources do we need?

★ What ideas do we have? Do we have to go out and find new ideas? Do we use our own R&D or do we buy in new technology?

★ What are the cash implications of our likely future plans? Is it likely that we need extra finance in order to be able to pursue our plans?

★ Can we 'sell' the strategic plans to the financial markets? And, thereby, are we able to raise any finance that we need?

There is no point setting off on the longer journey with excess baggage. On the other hand, you do need just the right amount of resources with which to run the business.

Investment in the long term will almost certainly be the outcome of such a strategic analysis. More capital investment will need to be injected into the business so that future plans can be achieved. We shall consider later the financial appraisal techniques that are used to evaluate long-term investment plans. Before that, we spend some time reviewing what we are doing now and what resources we have now, so that we are financially fit for the longer run. There is no point setting off on the longer journey with excess baggage. On the other hand, you do need just the right amount of resources with which to run the business.

Part Two, Immediate Actions, contains Chapters 4, 5 and 6 and looks at what we have now, and expect to have in the short term.

Long-term fitness is considered in Part Three, and consists of Chapters 7, 8, 9 and 10 which consider the longer term appraisal techniques.

IMMEDIATE ACTIONS

● ● ● ● ●

Financial appraisal techniques in the short term

How to use Part Two

Thisthis part of the Workout shows you how to assess the immediate activities of the business and the resources that it has to work with.

★ Use this part to check your knowledge of break-even analysis and of the difference between fixed and variable costs, in particular.

★ See how short-run decisions are influenced by the concept of the contribution made towards fixed costs and profit.

★ Develop practical methods that are designed to improve asset utilization – fixed assets and working capital.

★ Develop an understanding of the strategic implications of sound asset management on profitability, capital employed and upon cash flow.

Which products or services?

WARM-UP WORKOUT

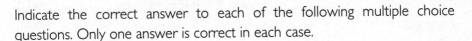

Indicate the correct answer to each of the following multiple choice questions. Only one answer is correct in each case.

1 The break-even point is reached when:

   (a) total revenue equals fixed costs

   (b) fixed costs equals variable cost

   (c) total revenue equals total cost.

2 A variable cost is a cost which:

   (a) stays the same whatever the level of production

   (b) increases with an increase in the level of production

   (c) amounts, per unit, to an ever-decreasing amount as production is increased.

3 A fixed cost is a cost which:

   (a) amounts, per unit, to an ever-decreasing amount as production is increased

   (b) increases with an increase in the level of production

   (c) equals revenue per unit of output.

4 The contribution per unit is equal to:

   (a) fixed costs per unit

   (b) the difference between total revenue and total variable cost

   (c) the difference between revenue per unit and variable cost per unit.

5 Pricing a particular product below its full cost but making a contribution towards overheads is, in principle, a good move provided there is no other work for the staff to do which will produce a higher contribution:

   (a) true

   (b) false.

Need for change to plans

Many day-to-day decisions are taken by managers reacting to events. This is not a criticism of managers – it is, after all, one of the reasons why managers exist – to take action when the unexpected happens. When sales are more or less than planned, when resources are in short supply, or when technology suddenly changes, managers have to make changes to plans in the short term . . . often making the best of the circumstances.

This leads to a range of similar types of decisions of which the main characteristic is that they are decisions that essentially affect only the short term. In the longer term, a different perspective may be taken. For example, if business increases, the short-term decision may be to work overtime; the longer-term decision might be to take on extra staff or even to invest in more facilities.

The key issue in short-run decision taking is whether or not costs can be altered in the short term. The type of cost that can be changed in the short run tends to be very similar to what the accountant calls a *variable* cost. On the other hand, *fixed* costs do not alter with the level of activity, at least in the short run. So before we go on to describe the types of short-term decisions faced by managers, we need to illustrate the importance of distinguishing between variable and fixed costs.

Break-even analysis

In accounting, some costs are regarded as fixed and some are regarded as variable. These terms have a particular meaning in accounting.

★ Fixed means that whatever the level of activity, the same costs will be spent within *the relevant range*.

★ Variable costs vary with output over the whole range of activity. The major assumption is that for each unit of output an equal and incremental cost is added.

The major assumption about a fixed cost is that it does not change within the expected level of activity. For example, the headcount of a particular department may be 20 people and their salaries, and other staff costs, will be fixed to a certain limited level of activity that they can achieve. Beyond that, further staff may have to be recruited. But, within the range of activity that those 20 people can cope with, the costs will not vary – they will be fixed.

The activity below asks you to determine which costs are fixed and variable from a list of common business expenses.

EXERCISE

WORKOUT

Which of the following costs would you regard as fixed and which as variable?

A telephone account
Salaries of office administrative staff
Marketing expenditure
Raw materials
Wages of shop-floor employees
Contracted-in staff
Interest on borrowing

Answer

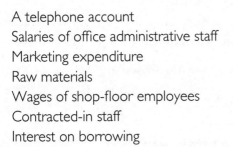

(a) *Fixed*
Telephone account*
Administrative salaries
Marketing expenditure*
Interest on borrowing

(b) *Variable*
Raw materials
Shop-floor wages – if
dependent upon output
Contracted-in staff

* There may be an element of variable cost included.

Graphical presentation of break-even analysis

Of course, both fixed and variable costs can be set out graphically in the classic break-even chart. In the figures which follow, 100 per cent capacity represents the relevant range. It would not be possible to increase production or other output beyond 100 per cent capacity without incurring further fixed costs. Strategic decisions probably have more to do with questions about exactly how a business increases its capacity outside, that is beyond, the level of full capacity. But as we suggested in the last chapter, short-term decisions do have an impact upon the strategic thinking of an organization. The break-even chart in Figure 4.1 indicates the following:

★ Variable costs increase at a constant rate for each unit of output (OF).

★ Fixed costs are added to variable costs to provide a total cost line for various levels of output (CD). The fixed costs are the same whether the production is nil (0C) or 100 per cent of capacity (FD).

★ Total revenue is drawn under the assumption that the sales price per unit of activity is constant, that is, the sales value of each additional unit of output is the same.

Thus all the lines in Figure 4.1 are straight lines. The break-even point is at AB, where the level of activity there makes neither a profit nor a loss.

In any business, we want to make a profit, so we are not particularly interested in the break-even point. Profit is made at levels of activity to

Figure 4.1　The break-even chart

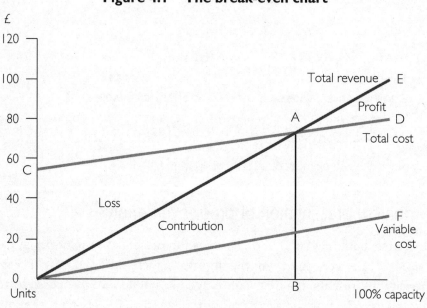

the right of the break-even point, and we want to make the maximum profit in relation to the amount of capital employed in the business. Profit is achieved after the break-even point, when the line AE (total revenue) is greater than the line AD (total costs).

WORKOUT

EXERCISE

From the break-even chart in Figure 4.1, estimate the following values:

(a) the percentage capacity at which the business illustrated breaks even

(b) the amount of profit (£s) at 100 per cent capacity

(c) the amount of loss (£s) at 50 per cent capacity.

Answer

(a) the business breaks even at 71.4 per cent capacity. (The computation of the break-even point is explained below, but you can probably see from the graph that the business breaks even at about 70 per cent capacity)

(b) the amount of profit at 100 per cent capacity amounts to £20,000

(c) the amount of loss at 50 per cent of capacity amounts to £15,000.

More about break-even analysis

What break-even analysis does is develop an understanding of the nature of the costs which have to be covered in order to make a profit. It explains such a lot about the way that we have to run our business. Break-even analysis really describes the underlying *behaviour of costs* – the distinction between fixed and variable costs – and the relationship between costs and revenue.

In principle, if all costs are *variable* and sales price is more than that cost, the business will always make a profit. This is shown in Figure 4.2a, where the profit is increasing at a constant rate – the more units

> **Break-even analysis really describes the underlying behaviour of costs – the distinction between fixed and variable costs – and the relationship between costs and revenue.**

Figure 4.2a   All costs are variable

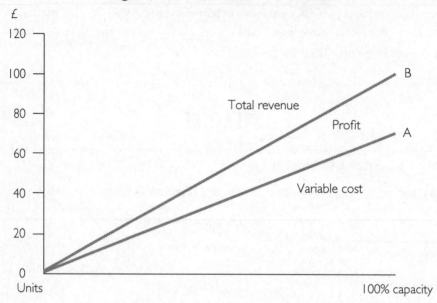

produced and sold the greater the total profit. On the other hand, as indicated in Figure 4.2b, given the same selling price of the product or service per unit, if all costs are *fixed*, at low levels of production and sales, a loss is made, before achieving profitability. If all the costs are

Figure 4.2b   All costs are fixed

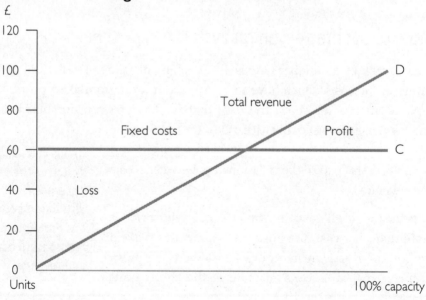

fixed, there is the potential to make more profit in total than if all the costs were variable. At full capacity, the total profit in Figure 4.2a is AB, which is less than the total profit in Figure 4.2b, which amounts to CD.

The concept of contribution

In Figure 4.1 the variable costs are drawn on the break-even chart first and fixed costs are added. This gives the total cost line CD. The virtue of drawing the diagram this way is that the area 0EF (the difference between sales revenue and variable costs) constantly increases as activity increases. The increase is constant because of the straight lines used in the diagram.

This area is known as the *contribution*. At the product or service level, it is the amount sales price exceeds variable cost per unit. At the cumulative level it is the contribution towards the fixed costs (until they are all covered) and then the profit. You can see the contribution cutting into the fixed costs then contributing towards profit as volume increases in Figure 4.1. At the break-even point, the contribution is exactly equal to the fixed costs. After that point, as activity increases to the right, the contribution contributes not only towards fixed costs, but also towards profit as indicated by the triangle AED.

The break-even point is calculated using the concept of contribution. Total fixed costs are divided by the contribution per unit or per £ of revenue to find out how many units or what level of sales revenue is needed to break even.

Contribution *per unit* is defined as:

Sales price per unit minus variable cost per unit

Contribution *per £ of revenue* is defined as:

$$\frac{\textbf{Sales price per unit minus variable cost per unit}}{\textbf{Sales price per unit}}$$

So the break-even point is:

in terms of units: $\dfrac{\textbf{Total fixed costs}}{\textbf{Sales price per unit minus variable cost per unit}}$

in terms of £ revenue: $$\frac{\text{Total fixed costs}}{\dfrac{\text{Sales price per unit minus variable cost per unit}}{\text{Sales price per unit}}}$$

EXERCISE

From the information provided below about Table Ltd calculate

(a) the break-even point in terms of sales revenue

(b) the break-even point in terms of volume (number of units)

(c) the break-even point in terms of percentage capacity

(d) the current level of profit

(e) the contribution per unit of production

(f) the contribution at the current level of output

(g) the contribution, if the business were to work at full capacity.

Information available from the management accounts of Table Ltd:

– Total fixed costs at current level of activity and full capacity £4,000,000

– Current total sales revenue £7,000,000

– Current volume of products sold 350,000 units

– Maximum volume of products that could be produced with current manufacturing facilities 450,000 units

– Variable costs of production £7 per unit.

Answer

(a) Break-even point in terms of sales revenue:
$$\frac{4,000,000}{\dfrac{20-7}{20}} = £6,153,846$$

(b) Break-even point in terms of volume:
$$\frac{4,000,000}{20-7} = 307,692 \text{ units}$$

(c) Break-even point in terms of percentage capacity:

$$\frac{\text{Volume of production for break even}}{\text{Maximum capacity}} = \frac{307,692}{450,000} = 68.4\%$$

(d) The current level of profit is:

	£
Sales revenue	7,000,000
Fixed costs	4,000,000
Variable costs	2,450,000
Profit	£550,000

(e) The contribution per unit of production:

	£
Sales price per unit	20
Variable cost per unit	7
Contribution per unit	£13

(f) The contribution at the current level of sales:

	£
Sales revenue	7,000,000
Variable costs	2,450,000
Current total contribution	£4,550,000

(g) Maximum contribution would be:

	£
Maximum sales revenue: 450,000 units at £20	9,000,000
Variable cost of maximum production: 450,000 units at £7	3,150,000
Maximum contribution with current facilities	£5,850,000

Decision making

It is to the right of the break-even line which is, of course, the area of the break-even chart where the business needs to be. This is where the company is making a profit. How much profit it ought to be making depends upon the aims and objectives of the company, the capital employed, the marketplace, and so on. This takes us back to budgeting.

Break-even analysis has to be set into an overall budgetary process. If there is not enough profit budgeted, it is necessary to review the forward plans to see whether any changes can be made. What this effectively means is that one or more of the lines in Figure 4.1 have to be altered. In the context of this simplistic break-even analysis, managers have just three factors to consider – represented by the three lines in the break-even chart:

★ **sales price** – in order to change the total revenue line

★ **variable costs** – in order to change, preferably decrease, the total variable cost line

★ **fixed costs** – in order to reduce the total fixed costs line.

Let us take a look at each of these lines of action in turn in a little more detail.

Changing sales price

Sales price may need to be changed in the light of a review of profitability. If no other changes can be made – no cost savings sought – the only way to improved budgeted profits may be to increase prices. It may be possible to increase volumes by *decreasing* prices, but normally less profit will be made if prices are reduced unless volume increases substantially. It is true that putting up prices will possibly lose business, depending upon the strength of competition and competitors' prices in the market, but often profit will increase when prices are increased.

For example, if a business makes a product where total revenue is £100, total fixed costs are £50 and total variable costs are £30, a profit of £20 will be made. If we assume that prices could be increased by 1 per cent without losing any volume of sales, volume would have to increase at least 3 per cent if prices were *reduced* by 1 per cent in order to make the same level of increased profit. The comparison is set out in Figure 4.3.

Changing variable costs

Variable costs, by and large, consist of raw materials or components or bought-in services. The way these can be reduced is by better purchasing or by more efficient use of those resources. It may be that by paying

Figure 4.3   Comparison between increasing and decreasing prices

	Present situation	Increasing price by 1%. No change in volume	Decreasing price by 1%. Volume increase of 3%
Sales revenue	100	101	102*
Fixed costs	50	50	50
Variable costs	30	30	31
Profit	20	21	21

* Calculated as follows: $100 \times .99 \times 1.03 = 102$

higher prices for the variable costs, greater efficiency of output can be achieved, so the choice of variable cost inputs is very often a technical issue which can only be resolved by managers who are very well acquainted with the operations of the business.

Changing fixed costs

Generally, speaking, the fixed costs of a business are those which are attacked most often. It is easy to put a limit on headcount, to stop or delay marketing expenditure, to cut training or to delay the purchase of new equipment (which affects depreciation charges). But, of course, any

We shall use the example of the budgetary processes of a UK-based computer systems company to illustrate the use of break-even analysis and the use of the contribution concept, in particular. The company is Callicom Systems plc and we shall consider a number of real decisions faced by one of its business units when it was budgeting for 1997. The business unit is CSS – Creative Software Systems – and it is a successful division of Callicom, employing 195 people. CSS provides both software systems and design support for the hardware sales divisions of Callicom, but also earns revenue by dealing direct with customers to provide specific user systems or to make amendments to them. Indeed the business unit is encouraged to take on outside work, because this ensures that it remains competitive and efficient. Figure 4.4 sets out the 1997 budget for CSS.

CASE STUDY

of these cuts may be detrimental to the long run wellbeing of the business. It may be possible to cut expenditure on fixed costs now, but, strategically speaking, this may have great disadvantages in the future.

Figure 4.4   CSS budget for 1997

	£000
Staff salaries	4,998
Overtime	392
Temporary salaries	23
Company pensions – company contribution	483
Social security	449
Total staff pay costs	**£6,345**
Company cars	369
Staff travel and subsistence	192
Canteen and welfare	80
Training	184
Total personnel-related costs	**£825**
Building maintenance	20
Telephone, postage and communications	1,345
Stationery and printing	228
Office furniture depreciation	59
Tenancy costs	505
Total facilities' costs	**£2,157**
Computer maintenance and modifications	425
Computer depreciation	1,207
Computer consumables	492
Bought out services	119
Total computer-related costs	**£2,243**
Total labour and overheads costs	**11,570**
Head office overhead allocation	**862**
Gross costs	**£12,432**
Total budgeted revenues	**13,832**
Profit	**£1,400**
Headcount	195

There may be longer-term ramifications from making changes to any of the variables – sales price, variable costs or fixed costs – as was discussed in the last chapter.

EXERCISE

Which, if any, of the costs in the 1997 budget may be regarded as variable? Remember variable costs strictly speaking, will be more or less, depending upon the volume of output.

Answer

The following costs of CSS could be said to be variable (that is, they change proportionately with the level of activity):

	£000
Overtime	392
Temporary salaries	23
Staff travel and subsistence	192
Computer consumables	492
Bought out services	119
Total variable costs	£1,218
Fixed costs therefore amount to	£11,214

Note: Some of the costs are, of course, variable in the sense that the business has the opportunity to *change* them – for example, training costs, which may or may not be spent at the discretion of management. A variable cost in the accounting sense is more strictly defined; as a cost which will increase as more *has* to be spent on it when more business is undertaken within the relevant range.

The answer to the above exercise suggests that most of the operating costs of CSS are fixed costs. These are the fixed costs which have to be covered by sufficient contribution before the CSS division makes a profit. After that any contribution will contribute towards profit. We can, therefore, perhaps make rather spurious calculations for CSS as follows. The break-even point formula is:

$$\frac{\text{Fixed costs}}{\dfrac{\text{Revenue} - \text{variable costs}}{\text{Revenue}}} = £ \text{ (sales at which business breaks even)}$$

CSS's break-even level of sales is thus:

$$\frac{£11,214,000}{\dfrac{£13,832,000 - £1,218,000}{£13,832,000}} = £12,296,816$$

This means that at £12.3 million sales CSS will break even, or, putting it another way, CSS has to achieve sales of £12.3 million before the business makes a profit. At sales of £13.8 million, as we can see from the budget, the budgeted profit amounts to £1.4 million.

The contribution approach to decision making

The concept of the contribution is very useful in making decisions about the products and services that a business might supply. The main principle is that, all other things being equal, providing a contribution towards fixed costs and profit is made in any particular activity, then it is worthwhile undertaking that work *provided that no better other work is available*. Better work, in this context, would be work that gave a higher contribution, taking into account the time and resources used to supply the product or service.

Such an approach is taken by some managers to price all products and services at variable cost plus a percentage to cover overheads and profit, so that some contribution is made, however small. But, generally speaking, work has to be taken at *full cost*, including a reasonable profit, so that we can be sure of covering the overheads at the end of the day. Once the overheads are met it may be reasonable to take work at a low contribution margin in order to increase profit but this is work taken 'at the margin'.

The reason for this argument is that the more units of a product or service that are made, the less each costs – *per unit*. See the example in Figure 4.5.

Figure 4.5 Unit cost

Units produced	100	150	200	250	300*
	£	£	£	£	£
Fixed costs	100	100	100	100	100
Variable costs	40	60	80	100	120
Total cost	140	160	180	200	220
Unit cost	1.40	1.07	0.90	0.80	0.73

* Full capacity

Full cost versus marginal cost pricing

This leads to arguments about full cost versus marginal cost pricing. Figure 4.6 indicates what happens if 10 per cent more business is undertaken at full cost. The profit increases by 80 per cent from £20 million to £36 million.

The original 'present situation' figures in Figure 4.6 (the first column of numbers) indicate that the business represented there is profitable. There is sufficient contribution in total to cover the fixed costs (£140 million) and make a profit (£20 million). If sales were increased by 10 per cent, the profit becomes £36 million. The company, in this case has maintained the selling price at its 'full cost' base.

Figure 4.6 A typical profit and full cost situation

	Present situation £m	10% increase in business (no price discounts) £m
Revenue	200	220
Costs: Fixed	140	140*
Variable	40	44
Profit	20	36
Units sold	100m	110m

* Assuming 10% extra business does not lead to an increase in fixed costs.

The managers of the business represented in Figure 4.6 will realize that the unit cost of the product has fallen from £1.80 each (£180 million costs divided by 100 million units) to £1.67 each (£184 million costs divided by 110 million units). This might encourage them to offer the product at a discount. It might be very attractive for the company to offer a discount for *extra* sales in these circumstances.

Figure 4.7   A Typical profit and marginal cost situation

	Present situation £m	25% increase in business (40% price discount) £m
Revenue	200	230
Costs: Fixed	140	140*
Variable	40	50
Profit	20	40
Units sold	100m	125m
Unit cost	£1.80	£1.52

* Assuming 25% extra business does not lead to an increase in fixed costs.

In Figure 4.7, a 40 per cent discount on price encourages a further 25 per cent in the volume of sales. The 40 per cent discount has only been given to the extra customers, not the original ones. In this event, profit doubles from £20 million to £40 million, so the effect of taking on the 'marginal' business looks very attractive. It is, however, marginal business, because the extra business has paid a price below the full cost of the product, which is shown to be £1.52 per unit in Figure 4.7 (£190 million costs divided by 125 million units). The price charged for the extra sales, less a 40 per cent discount, would amount to only £1.20 per unit. More profit is made because the fixed cost overheads are covered by the sales of the 100 million units at the regular selling price of £2.00 per unit. The extra sales do not incur any additional fixed costs so the extra profit equals the extra contribution made.

	£m
Extra sales 25 million units at £1.20	30
Extra variable costs 25 million × £0.40	10
Extra contribution	£20

Now, 20 per cent of the market has the firm's goods at 40 per cent discount! This may have serious long-term implications. Not all work can be taken on that basis, for two reasons:

1. Not all the overheads will be recovered if too much work is taken at low margins.

2. You may undermine prices in the current market generally, which may decrease all margins.

Two major business decisions: mix and pricing

Having developed the usefulness of determining the difference between fixed and variable costs, we shall move on to examples of the kinds of *strategic* decisions that have a contribution aspect. They are:

★ product mix decisions

★ pricing.

We shall use the information we have from the Callicom Systems case study and other examples to illustrate these two strategic decisions.

Product mix decisions

In the case of CSS, the managers will be well aware of the fact that, as well as achieving sales revenue of £13.8 million, the other major task will be to match the headcount of 195 people to the requirements of meeting those sales. What this means is that work will have to be scheduled so that each person has a reasonable workload for the year. This is obviously extremely difficult and it may well be that the work that is actually undertaken, that is the sales that are actually made, is as much based upon the people that are available, when they are available, than the sales opportunities that the business actually achieves.

Work flow scheduling is obviously of great importance to a software design business – and indeed to many other companies too. The final mix of contracts (products) that the business undertakes will depend upon the contribution made by the best use of the staff resources available. Remember, the contribution is the difference between the contract price and the direct costs involved in it and it is management's sales effort that aims to maximize the contributions from contracts in this way. The contribution approach gives the managers much more flexibility than simply using an hourly rate for staff and operating costs.

For example, let us imagine that in one of the teams of software designers in CSS, there are ten employees. Let us assume that the cost of each employee, *including overheads*, is £70 per hour. The manager of this team of ten people will want it to work as effectively as possible. What does this mean? It means making the highest contribution towards the £70 per hour for each employee.

WORKOUT

EXERCISE

Assume that over the next three months the ten employees could work, allowing for holidays, training, sickness and so on, a total of 3,500 chargeable hours (350 hours each). Chargeable hours are those which are charged out for work for a client or to other divisions of Callicom Systems. During the next three months the projects this team could work on are:

	Hours	Direct costs £	Price quoted £	Contribution £
Job 1	1,500	20,000	130,000	110,000
2	1,500	12,000	120,000	108,000
3	2,000	43,000	200,000	157,000
4	1,200	13,000	101,000	88,000

What is the optimal product mix?

Answer

An exact match of the number of hours available could be attained with Jobs 1 and 3 or Jobs 2 and 3. The combination of Jobs 1 and 3 gives the higher contribution.

There may be other alternatives: for example, Jobs 1, 2 and 4 could be completed if 700 hours of overtime were allowed and were possible.

Depending on the overtime pay, this alternative would give a contribution of £306,000 less overtime payments. This would have to be carefully compared with Jobs 1 and 3 where the contribution amounts to £267,000, but with no need for overtime.

So the optimal product mix is established by finding out which mix of jobs is likely to give the highest contribution towards fixed costs and, hopefully, profit. What about the strategic implications of such product mix decisions? In the above example, you might feel that the optimal mix decision has only a short-term perspective. Once the current period's product mix is decided, there is nothing more that can be done until the next opportunity to decide what to do comes along. But the next exercise asks you to consider whether there are any strategic implications of the apparently short-run decision about the best product mix.

EXERCISE

. . . .

What are the strategic implications of the above analysis?

WORKOUT

Answer

Obviously, much would depend upon other factors:

★ the need to maintain a position in the market and not lose jobs to competitors

★ the possibility of managing all the jobs with the partial use of outside contractors, overtime, or even taking on more staff

★ the possibility of delaying one or more of the contracts to the following three months.

Another example of product mix

You can check your understanding of the product mix decision, and the contribution approach to business decisions by considering the dilemma set out in the following exercise.

WORKOUT

EXERCISE

A company has three products A, B and C. Revenue and cost information about each of the products is as follows:

	A £000	B £000	C £000
Sales	100	200	250
Variable costs	60	100	105
Contribution	40	100	145
Fixed costs	50	80	110
Profit (loss)	(£10)	£20	£35

The company's accountant argues that product A should be dropped. What do you think?

Answer

Product A makes a contribution of £40,000 towards the overheads and profit of the company. Dropping A would make the company £40,000 worse off unless one or more of the following changes could be made:

(a) the resources which are used to make A could be used more productively to make B or C or another, more profitable, product. This would have to assume that the further production of B or C or the other product could be sold.

(b) the resources used to make A could be reduced. Fixed costs would have to be reduced by at least £10,000, in order to avoid product A's loss.

(c) long-term considerations would need to be brought into account: would the dropping of product A have ramifications for the marketing of products B and C?

Pricing

Prices of products or services are based on the cost of providing them to the customer plus a margin for profit. In simple terms, this means calculating the costs from available budgets of fixed and variable costs, and adding a percentage for profit. But because some of the costs are fixed, much depends upon the *volume* of business, as to exactly what the cost base is. Figure 4.5 illustrated how as the cost per unit decreased, the more units of production there were to spread the fixed costs over.

Consequently, when pricing decisions are made, some estimate of the level of activity has to be assumed. A factory plant needs to consider exactly how many productive hours are feasible and likely. Feasible hours will depend upon the number of shifts worked, tooling time (if production lines are changed during the year) and periods of close down for holidays and maintenance. Likely time will depend upon the need to run the plant to produce the number of units required to meet market demand. There is no point running a plant at 100 per cent capacity if only 80 per cent of that output can be sold.

EXERCISE

. . . .

How many 'productive' hours do you work? How many 'productive' hours does the department or business in which you work perform as a proportion of the total hours available?

WORKOUT

Answer

It is obviously impossible to say what your level of activity is without a thorough knowledge of your business – the hours available and how 'productive' hours might be measured. Here are a few guidelines for different types of business:

(a) factory production lines may well aim to be active 80–90 per cent of total hours available. When they are running, they may well be running at 100 per cent capacity, but there will be 'down time', when there is a change-over of jobs, machine breakdowns and time for maintenance which may well add 10 per cent or more of the total hours available.

(b) a hotel will aim to have as high an occupancy rate as possible – ideally again 100 per cent, but probably achieving only around 60 per cent. Prices will have to be set – to recover the fixed costs of the hotel – based on 60 per cent occupancy. They will therefore need to be much higher than if the hotel expected to achieve, say, 80 per cent occupancy.

Because of the number of rooms that are often vacant, many hotels resort to marginal pricing; very cheap room rates, which make some contribution to the fixed costs. Such low-cost pricing can be seen to erode the full-cost business, so the buzz words in the hotel industry are 'yield management' (room occupancy percentage multiplied by the average room rate).

(c) those of the service sector which are essentially people based – consultants, accountants, trainers, maintenance engineers, software houses – have to keep a close eye on the number of hours charged out to clients or charged to projects that will eventually be paid for by clients. Software engineers, for example, aim to have 60–70 per cent of their time charged out to contracts. The remainder of their time will be spent reviewing new equipment and systems, training, on holiday and, perhaps, waiting for new work.

CASE STUDY

Pricing a service contract

As an example of pricing in the service sector, return to the information we have about CSS, the business unit of Callicom Systems. CSS was asked to quote for a systems design job in America to be completed in 1997; not as additional work, but as part of the work the division would be doing within its budget targets for 1997.

There are two steps in this analysis as to the price at which CSS should offer to do the work:

★ First, we have to calculate an hourly rate to charge for the engineers that are going to be used on the contract. This charge-out rate would have to include the costs of those staff in the division who do not work directly on particular contracts, such as administrative staff, managers and so on.

★ Second, an estimate would need to be made of the hours required to complete the contract. The base cost of the contract would then be the estimated hours multiplied by the cost per hour of the software team.

EXERCISE

· · · · · · · · ·

WORKOUT

Making the *major simplifying assumption* that all systems design staff are of equal standing – in terms of their skills, experience and so on – at what hourly rate should they be charged out, if Callicom's objectives for the business unit are to be achieved?

The budget for CSS was provided in Figure 4.4. You will also need to have the following information in order to answer this question.

CSS has 165 systems design staff (other employees are management staff and administrators) and the annual hours of work for the design staff are:

Estimated total hours per technical employee per week	35 hours
Total working year	48 weeks
Total annual available hours	1,680
less annual non-chargeable travelling time to visit customers,	
awaiting work, etc.	–340
annual non-chargeable time; sickness, training, etc.	–170
Net productive hours for pricing (per technician)	1170

Note: overtime is paid after 35 hours work per week have been worked. If overtime is paid, it is paid at the rate of £28 per hour.

Answer

The hourly rate that systems design staff should be charged at is calculated as follows:

$$\frac{\text{Total labour and overhead costs plus head office overhead allocation}}{\text{Number of chargeable staff} \times \text{productive bonus per person}}$$

$$= \frac{£11,570,000 + £862,000}{165 \times £170}$$

$$= £64.40 \text{ per hour}$$

In pricing a particular contract, estimated direct costs would need to be added plus 1/9th to achieve the profit margin of approximately 10 per cent on revenue that CSS seek to achieve in 1997.

EXERCISE

• • • • • • • • •

It is estimated that the work on the American contract will take 8,500 staff hours to complete. The job may be commenced on 1 May but has to be completed by 31 July 1997. There are penalty clauses in the contract of $2,000 per day for non-completion in 13 weeks' time.

Assuming that the work is well within the competence of CSS's staff, at what price should the contract be tendered for?

(a) You are required to offer a price for this job in a very competitive environment.

(b) In which currency do you offer the contract? (You may take it that the exchange rate is US$1.50 to £1.00.)

Answer

The simple answer to this question is that the price that can be quoted is:

	£
Contract hours charged at hourly rate:	
8,500 hours at £64.40	547,400
Profit: 1/9th	60,822
Contract price	£608,222
Contract price in $*	$912,333

* The job would have to be quoted in US dollars to an American customer.

Note: An overall, average hourly recovery rate has been used in this question. Consequently, only a very rough costing has been used as the basis for the quotation for the contract. Further detail might be used in calculating the bid price for the contract. For example, the various grades of employee to be used on the project could be assigned different recovery rates. Their budgeted time on the contract would then be multiplied out to establish a more accurate contract bid price.

Further consideration of the bid price

Let us imagine that CSS know that a competitor has quoted $800,000 for the job. Should CSS take on the competition and offer a price below that of the competitor's?

If, say, they offered a contract price of $750,000, the contribution towards CSS's profits would be around £456,000:

	£
Revenue: $750,000 at $1.50 : £1.00	500,000
Variable costs: approx 8.8% of revenue*	44,000
Contribution	£456,000

* In an answer to an earlier exercise, about what were the variable costs of CSS, the variable costs were shown to be approximately 8.8 per cent of revenue.

If CSS is working below capacity it might be worthwhile taking on such a contract which makes a contribution of £456,000 towards the division's overheads – which are being spent in any case. It is better to undertake the work at such a price – and make the contribution of £456,000 – rather than reject the contract, but still have to pay the overheads, and 8,500 hours of cost, which would still have to be paid (amounts to £547,000 (8,500 hours at £64.40)). It is much better to make the contribution of £456,000 than not to do the contract and make no contribution.

This is so provided no other work is available which will provide a greater contribution. Furthermore, with the American contract there may be other, additional overheads which need to be considered before a final decision was made as to which price to offer the contract at. For example, for such a large contract there may well be further costs for:

★ additional staff that have to be taken on in order to complete the contract

★ extra travelling to visit the customer in America

★ abnormal or expensive computing time

★ specialist manuals or training for the contract

★ abnormal hardware modifications.

The counter argument to offering the contract at below full cost (which is $912,333) is that, if the contract were accepted at the lower price, CSS would be undertaking work which is of a lower profit margin. From a strategic point of view, this may be a dangerous decision. You may be keeping employees more fully employed, but you might be undercutting your own market. If other customers begin to know that you are doing work for another company at below full cost prices, they may also want their work done at that rate. It is probably safe to offer work which makes a contribution but not a profit in overseas markets (although this is probably against GATT arrangements) because you are unlikely to be undercutting your home market business. However, one has to remember that we are living in a global market and it is quite likely that customers will know what is being charged in several countries in the world and will be aware that you are willing to undercut prices in America but not in the UK.

Concluding points

This chapter has concentrated on the short term. Short-term activity does have an impact upon strategy because sometimes it precludes longer, term strategy and, in any case, it sends messages to the market as to what the company is up to. Strategic decisions are probably more to do with changing the relevant range of activity (increasing or decreasing it) rather than what goes on within it. Strategy sets out the stall and short run activity achieves the results.

The contribution concept can be used in all sorts of ways to help managers decide upon the best course of action, given the resources at hand. It is particularly useful in two major management decisions:

★ the pricing of products and services

★ the management of optimal product mix and resource utilization.

What do we have to work with? – fixed assets

The impact of the efficient use of assets on the return on capital

....

Utilization and control of fixed assets

....

Effect of lease versus buy on the utilization of assets ratio

....

The management of intangible assets

....

The treatment of brand values and goodwill in company balance sheets

The efficient use of assets

The assumption is made throughout this Workout that business is seeking to maximize the return to the providers of the capital in the business. The return on capital employed measures how well we are doing in that respect. The previous chapter looked at the decisions that have to be constantly made in order to maximize the profit that the business can achieve. In this chapter and the next, we turn to the other half of the calculation of the return on capital employed – the amount tied up in the assets of the business.

The efficient use of assets will have an important effect on the return on capital employed. Small improvements in the utilization of assets will have a dramatic effect on the return on capital employed. For example, if the profit margin on sales is 7 per cent and the asset utilization ratio is 2.0 times, the return on capital employed will be 14 per cent (2 x 7 per cent). If the asset utilization ratio could be improved to, say, 2.3 times, the return on capital employed would increase to 16.1 per cent (2.3 x 7 per cent). This may not seem a great deal but small percentage changes in finance have a great effect. On the stock market, an improvement of 2 per cent in the return on capital employed will be highly regarded.

The asset utilization ratio is calculated by dividing the sales revenue achieved by the assets employed in the business required to provide that level of sales. The assets may be plant and machinery for a manufacturer, or equipment to provide a service in the service sector or distribution vehicles and warehousing in the distribution sector, and so on. The more that these assets can produce or the more services that can be provided with them, the better the asset utilization ratio.

Of course, one of the ways to increase the asset utilization is to sell more! The next exercise asks you to consider the implications of that.

EXERCISE

· · · · · · · · ·

If the business objective is set to expand sales, more or less at all costs, in order to use assets more effectively, can you think of any financial problems that might arise from that policy?

Answer

A number of financial problems may occur if more and more sales are made without due care.

1   The business may not be able to produce the goods sold or to keep up with the demand for the service offered. This may lead to urgent action to acquire more facilities which may lead to cash flow problems in the short run.

2   If products are bought in to help, these may be more expensive or not of the right quality, which will have an effect on the profitability of the company.

3   Higher than expected sales may mean that more cash is tied up in working capital than was originally forecast. The company could be faced with cash flow problems keeping up with the demand.

4   If sales are expanded 'at all costs', the margin of profit may well become accepted as the norm in the market. Increasing that margin later may be difficult to do.

The alternative to selling more is to control the amount of assets required to provide the goods or services. Careful planning should be undertaken to ensure that whatever assets are needed are available, but no more than that. This is because the fewer the assets held, the less is the amount of finance required. Each asset owned by the business has to be acquired, using the capital supplied by the owners of the business. The fewer the assets, the less the finance and so the profits made by the company are shared between fewer providers of finance – so each of their shares is worth proportionately more.

The control of assets

In the recession of the 1990s, a lot of effort was put into the careful analysis and management of exactly what assets are required by a business. In the 1980s, it could be said that the greater concentration had been on margins – on pricing policy and on efficient manufacturing from the point of view of cost – in order to maximize the profit margin as a percentage of sales. Obviously, not everything that could be done to reduce costs has been done but managers find it more and more difficult to make inroads into the cost base. Margins have also been squeezed by very competitive pricing during the 1990s. So, as there is not much that can be done to improve the profit margin on sales, the attack has moved to the other factor in the return on capital employed – the utilization of assets.

Although assets can be reduced – they can be sold off – the better way to control the amounts of assets is not to own them in the first place! Careful planning will ensure that the assets we have are the minimum we need to run the business. Surplus assets will reduce the asset utilization ratio and the return on capital employed. Furthermore, each asset held has to be funded by the providers of finance.

But what are the assets? How can the asset utilization ratio be improved? Let us look a little more closely at each type of asset. When we are clear what these assets are, we will be able to assess whether there are surplus assets or not. It is in the balance sheet that we find what assets the company has to work with. The assets are listed there as:

★ Fixed assets: Tangible assets

★ Fixed assets: Intangible assets

★ Current assets: Stocks

★ Current assets: Debtors.

Let us look at each of these in turn. The management of fixed assets will be considered in this chapter; the control of current assets and 'working capital' will be discussed in Chapter 6.

Tangible fixed asset utilization

Of major strategic importance for fixed assets is whether or not the assets in the business are being used effectively. Are they used to their full potential? Here is a very simple example.

What about the annual utilization rate of an office desk? Is it used to its full potential? A desk is, arguably, actually used for less than 15 per cent of the total number of hours that it is available for use! In a seven or eight hour day, taking into account time away from the desk for meetings, meal breaks, coffee breaks and so on, an office worker is probably not using – or even sitting at – the desk for more than an average of five hours each working day. That is, about 25 hours a week. Taking into account holidays, sickness, public holidays and so on, the typical office worker may be at work for no more than 47 or 48 weeks a year – which means that the employee is actually sitting at the desk for no more than about 1,200 hours per year. As there are 8,760 hours altogether in a year (24 hours x 365 days), the office desk is being used for less than 15 per cent of the time. Even worse than that, the computer terminal that the office worker uses has an even lower utilization rate than that of the desk upon which it sits!

It is true that we do not consider such low utilization in practice because the hours an asset is used is taken as a proportion of the number of working hours available. In the case of the desk, if it were only being used for 25 hours out of, say, a 35 hour week, we would say that the utilization rate was around 70 per cent, not taking account of weeks off for holidays, sickness and so on!

There are some assets which are so costly that they have to be used much more effectively. These facilities will be run non-stop so that the most use can be made of them. The exercise below asks you to consider why some assets have to be used non-stop.

EXERCISE

Why do some assets have to be used continuously? Can you think of any reasons why they should be?

Answer

There may be a number of reasons why assets should be used non-stop. The following are the reasons that we are aware of:

★ Because of the huge initial capital cost of the asset, it has to be used constantly to make it economically viable. An example of such an asset is oil wells served from a floating, sea platform. The cost of such marine platforms – sometimes thousands of millions of US dollars – is such that they are worked 24 hours each day.

★ Because of the costs of closing down the plant and recommissioning. There may also be technical reasons why the facilities have to be used constantly; for example, in the case of the oil field, the oil cannot feasibly be turned off.

★ Because of the activities of competitors in the market. If very expensive assets are being utilized 24 hours each day by competitors, their cost base will be reduced, their products will be cheaper on the market and they will gain market share, simply because of the higher utilization rate of the assets they are employing.

Hopefully, the example of the utilization rate of the office desk is not true of expensive plant in a factory or of the major items of equipment in an office environment. Much manufacturing plant and equipment is used for 80–90 per cent of the time, the remaining 10–20 per cent being used for maintenance and changing over jobs. Many computer systems are operated on the basis of 24 hours each day. During the night shift, backing up takes place and batch data processing is carried out in order to leave the mainframe freer for access and for managing the network during the day.

The next exercise illustrates the use of assets and the strategic implications of doing so.

EXERCISE

• • • • • • • • •

Consider the pros and cons from a *strategic* point of view of the following alternative asset purchasing opportunities available to a haulage contractor. Although information is given to you about running costs, do not consider just the financial aspects of the question. The financial information is given to you to highlight the financial issues, that is, which policy will be most profitable! But what are the wider business issues to be considered in making the choice between the two assets?

The haulage firm has a major client which contracts out its distribution and work for that client takes top priority. The contractor has the choice between acquiring one large vehicle or two smaller trucks. Either alternative can carry the same volume and weight of goods when the business is fully engaged by clients. Often the business is fully employed, because it has one large customer who takes up the whole capacity of the lorries when required, but this is not all the time. So we have:

★ one large lorry – which is not always fully utilized by the major client, *or*

★ two smaller trucks – which could generate other income when not required for the major client.

The larger truck's running costs amount to £1.37 per mile; the running costs of each of the smaller trucks is £1.64 per mile. These are the variable costs of running the vehicles. Charges are made to the client on the basis of tonnage carried per mile – so that if a lorry is not full, it may well not cover the appropriate proportion of fixed costs as well as the running costs with the earnings from its load.

Which strategy should the contractor employ – two vehicles or one?

Answer

It is assumed that the major customer is to be served at all costs because the haulage contractor does not want to lose that business. The accounting and finance criteria for the decision would revolve around the utilization of the fixed cost elements in the two alternatives as well as the difference in the variable running costs of each vehicle. As we saw in the previous chapter when looking at pricing decisions, it is crucial that sufficient total contribution is made to cover total fixed costs so that a profit is made. If the work provided by the major client is enough to cover all the fixed costs of the business, taking into account any variable cost, then it may be best from the financial point of view simply to acquire the larger truck – that is, after all, a truck that is capable of doing whatever work comes from the major client. If the lorry is available sometimes for other work, the contribution from that work will contribute towards the profit of the business – and its contribution per mile is greater than that of the smaller vehicles!

On the other hand, if the managers of the firm are at all uncertain of the volume of business to be placed with them by their major client, their strategy may be improved by having the option of two vehicles. The more variable each day the size of loads, the more flexible their response to the business should be. A small load could be carried by one of the smaller trucks. This will be at a higher cost per mile, which would contribute less to the fixed costs, but the business has the opportunity to earn extra revenue with the other vehicle. This possibility would not be available if the large lorry only was used.

When is asset utilization a strategic issue?

Asset utilization on a day-to-day basis is arguably not a strategic matter. Assets that the company holds should be used as efficiently as possible and, as in the case of the haulage contractor in the exercise above, they should ideally be flexible enough to be used as much as possible. In this way the asset utilization ratio will be as high as possible. There are strategic issues surrounding the tactical use of assets; for example, which customers or clients to satisfy first when it is physically impossible to provide goods and services to meet all demands on the equipment. But, generally speaking, the day-to-day utilization of assets is simply an operational matter.

The fact that the company owns the assets, however, is certainly the result of an earlier *strategic* decision. The strategic question will have arisen when the decision was taken to buy the asset in question in the first place, or when it was decided to replace the assets presently owned. That was the time when a *capital investment decision* was made. It is such

There is no point in acquiring new assets for expansion or in replacing assets, if the decision is to be taken to wind down a particular line of business.

occasions which provide an ideal opportunity to review the longer-term strategy of the business. There is no point in acquiring new assets for expansion or in replacing assets, if the decision is to be taken to wind down a particular line of business. So the decision to buy fixed assets should be carefully linked to a company's strategy.

The techniques of capital investment appraisal which facilitate the decision to acquire new assets are covered in Chapters 9 and 10. We shall emphasize there, again, that the investment decision to purchase new assets must take into consideration the corporate strategic objectives.

Improving asset utilization

We have spent some time looking at the importance of improving asset utilization. The following is a list of methods and techniques that have been, and are being, used to improve the use of assets and thereby the asset utilization ratio. Some of these activities are one-off, others are on-going:

★ manufacturing process re-engineering. Reconsideration of production processing practices

★ research and innovation to make more efficient and effective use of assets and ultimately to develop production processes which use cheaper (to purchase and to run) capital equipment

★ work flow scheduling. Having a constant flow of work is essential if high levels of asset utilization are to be maintained. There is no point if a production line is efficient but it takes too long to change over lines or to obtain new business at the end of a contract for a long production run.

Lease or buy

One very quick way to improve asset utilization is to lease an asset, rather than buy it. This has the effect of taking the fixed asset off the lessee's balance sheet and the asset utilization figure dramatically improves! Figure 5.1 shows the implications of leasing on the asset utilization ratio for a company that leases 50 per cent of its fixed assets.

Figure 5.1   Effect of leasing on the asset utilization ratio

	Fixed assets acquired	50% fixed assets leased
Balance sheet totals	£000	£000
Fixed assets	200	100
Current asset	100	100
	300	200
Sales revenue	560	560
Asset utilization ratio	1.87 times	2.80 times

There are, of course, a number of factors that have to be considered before a business leases rather than purchases its capital assets.

1. There *might* be an adverse effect on the profit. This will depend upon the relative cost of the lease compared to the cost of financing the purchase and depreciating the asset.

2. There will be the impact upon taxation. The lessor may be able to obtain an advantageous tax position that is not available to the operating company.

3. Increased leasing will be regarded as further borrowing by lenders and the interest rate chargeable on other borrowing may be increased because of the extra financial risk. This makes the leasing arrangements more expensive than perhaps might appear at first sight. However, leasing may allow other borrowing to be reduced, because the asset is no longer to be acquired.

It is fair to say that the accountancy profession, which is the main body responsible for drawing up accounts, is currently considering the rules relating to leased assets. Although operating leases are not shown on the balance sheet, finance leases, where effectively the company is buying the asset through the leasing arrangement, are shown on the balance sheet. It is very likely in the near future that the accounting rules will change so that operating leases will also be shown, at their capital cost, on users' balance sheets. This will mean that hiding assets 'off balance sheet' will no longer be an option that businesses will have open to them.

Such a move would return us to sensible financial management considerations, rather than being driven by accounting rules. *Leasing should be seriously considered as a strategic option*, not because of its off balance sheet advantage but because it

★ is an alternative means of borrowing

★ ties the user into the supplier, who has to keep the asset working in order get the lease payments

★ might be more tax effective to lease

★ might be easier to persuade a supplier to upgrade an asset if it is leased.

Does your business unit need to own all the assets you use in your operations? Have you considered the leasing alternative?

[REMEMBER: leasing is not necessarily cheaper – the cost of leasing is probably much the same as owning the asset – but a leased asset may be easier to upgrade and it may make your return on capital employed look better!]

Utilization of intangible fixed assets

The term intangible fixed assets represents the value of the business over and above the balance sheet value of its tangible fixed assets and working capital. The total of the value of assets shown in the balance sheet is usually less than the market value of the whole business. The market value of the business is the value of all the shares quoted on a stock exchange or the price you would have to pay for the whole business to acquire it. The reason for the difference between the market value of the business and that of its assets is that there is goodwill in the business which is not recorded as part of the assets.

Accountants are reluctant to put a value on goodwill because in order to value it you have to value the business as a whole – then deduct the value of the tangible assets to find the value of goodwill. As you will know from the stock market, the value of a business fluctuates constantly; share prices go down as well as up. Therefore, if the value of the business is fluctuating, so is the value of goodwill, and accountants could never be very sure of the value that might be placed upon it.

Some companies, none the less, have made an attempt to value their goodwill, or at least part of it. In the UK, a number of companies have made an estimate of the value of their brands. The value of branded goods is part of the value of goodwill of a company producing them. The cumulative brand value is calculated based upon the brand premiums of each individual product in the market place. The brand premium is the difference between the price a particular product sells for in the market place and the price of an unbranded, but similar, product.

When you see the value of intangible assets in the balance sheet, it usually represents the value of goodwill or brands *acquired* by the company from another business. Goodwill arises when an acquiring company pays more for the tangible assets than their fair value. This is usually the case of course because, as we have said above, the value of a whole business is probably worth more than the sum of the assets in the balance sheet. Figure 5.2 shows the accounting of the takeover of company B by company A and exactly how goodwill arises. Company A pays £400,000 of company A's shares to the shareholders of company B. B's tangible assets are combined with those of company A in the combined companies' balance sheet. The balancing figure of £200,000 is goodwill because A paid £400,000 for assets which in B's balance sheet were shown as £200,000.

Figure 5.2   Goodwill following a takeover

Company A Balance Sheet

	£000		£000
Shareholders' funds	5,000	Assets	5,000

Company B Balance Sheet

	£000		£000
Shareholders' funds	200	Assets	200

Combined A and B Balance Sheet

	£000		£000
Shareholders' funds	5,400	Assets	5,200
		Goodwill	200
	£5,400		£5,400

Management of intangible fixed assets

How do we best manage this intangible asset when we have argued throughout this chapter that the aim of sound strategic management is to minimize the assets in the balance sheet in order to improve the return on capital employed? There are some arguments for the inclusion of intangible assets in the balance sheet. It may well be that in future years, the accounting practice will be to attempt to value goodwill. After all, from a strategic perspective, the objective of sound corporate management is the maximization of the value of the goodwill of the business. Senior management should be ensuring that the value of goodwill – and therefore of the business as a whole – is growing year on year. How can they find out if they are doing this if accountants do not make some attempt to value the goodwill of the business?

> *The objective of sound corporate management is the maximization of the value of the goodwill of the business.*

A number of reasons can be suggested why management like to see goodwill in the balance sheet – in spite of the fact that they might have concern about the effect adding goodwill to the balance sheet has on reducing the return on capital employed.

1. It might be felt that bringing goodwill and brand values into the balance sheet, underpins the share price better than trying to improve the return on capital employed by excluding them. Managers may feel that they are less vulnerable to takeover if the full value of the intangibles is shown in the balance sheet. At least, they will argue, a high price will have to be paid for the company by any potential acquiring company.

2. Companies do purchase and sell brand names and other intangible assets such as trade marks and intellectual property rights. The value of these intangibles could be managed, like any other asset, in order to maximize the benefit from them. If their value was registered in the balance sheet, the success of the management of these assets would be reflected in their valuation. The increase or decrease in value could be associated with the amount of, and success of, marketing and advertising that have to be undertaken to maintain or increase the value of the intangibles.

3. The amount of intangible assets in the balance sheet will increase the balance sheet value of shareholders' equity and consequently gearing or leverage ratios (debt/equity ratios) will be reduced.

4. It is possible, in some countries, to use the accounting rules regarding goodwill to 'improve' the apparent return on capital employed. In the UK, the accounting rules allow goodwill to be written off to reserves. The effect of this is shown in Figure 5.3 where the goodwill on the acquisition of company B by company A, as was the case in Figure 5.2, is written off to the equity reserves of company A immediately after the takeover. The outcome of this is to reduce the combined companies' capital employed from £5.4m to £5.2m. If the combined profit of the two companies is, say, £800,000, the return on capital employed improves from 14.8 per cent to 15.4 per cent.

Figure 5.3   Goodwill written off to reserves

Combined A & B Balance Sheet			
	£000		£000
Shareholders' funds	5,400	Assets	5,200
Goodwill written off	(200)		
	£5,200		£5,200

Conclusion

Fixed assets need to be used efficiently. There is no value in holding assets that are not used effectively in the business. Any surplus assets should be disposed of.

Managers will have to decide for themselves whether or not to include intangible fixed assets in the balance sheet or not. It may be that managers seek to 'manage' their intangible fixed assets by actively seeking to maximize their value on the face of the balance sheet. In this way the return on capital employed will be less, but a more realistic value of capital employed will be shown in the balance sheet.

What do we have to work with? – working capital

The importance of effective use of working capital

The choice between having a lot of working capital versus minimal working capital

The problem of having too much working capital: on profitability and on cash flow

How to keep control of stocks

How to keep control of debtors

Relations with suppliers and with customers

Managing amounts owed to suppliers

Managing cash

WARM-UP WORKOUT

WORKOUT

1 Does working capital increase or decrease when the business grows?

2 The following figures have been extracted from the balance sheet of Stones Ltd, a small producer of garden furniture, for the two years to 31 December 1995 and 1996.

	1995 £000	1996 £000
Stock of raw materials	68	67
Stock of finished goods	128	144
Debtors (accounts receivable)	252	278
Creditors (accounts payable)	151	171

Has the working capital of Stones increased or decreased over the year?

3 What can be done to reduce the amounts tied up in debtors (accounts receivable)?

4 What can be done to reduce the amounts tied up in stocks or inventories?

5 Do you feel that it is best to leave it as long as possible to pay suppliers what is owed to them?

The effective use of working capital

In the previous chapter, we showed the importance of using the fixed assets – whether they be tangible or intangible – as effectively as possible. This is because every penny tied up in assets has to be financed. Some person or some institution has to put up money to fund the investment, and then a return is expected on it. The same argument can be made for working capital. For the same reasons, we want as little working capital as possible.

Working capital consists of the amounts of money a business has *at any point in time* tied up in:

★ stocks or inventories which may be
  - raw materials
  - work in progress or contracted work unfinished
  - finished goods awaiting a customer to buy them

★ debtors or receivables (accounts receivable)

★ creditors or payables (accounts payable).

The total of working capital is: *stock* plus *debtors* minus *creditors*.

The actual amount of working capital required very much depends upon your business and your experience of it. In terms of deciding how much working capital you need, you are torn between the two extremes:

★ a high level of service to customers who can buy anything you have to offer from stock at any time (which means your keeping high levels of stock) and who you do not chase for payment (which means you may have high amounts owed by customers)

★ a minimal amount tied up in working capital by keeping stocks down and debtors at a reasonable level.

If a company has too much tied up in working capital, it will, as with fixed assets, have to find more capital than it needs. But the problem is even worse than that. If a business is trying to grow, doing so without control of working capital will mean it is climbing uphill with a burden on its back. The best way to illustrate why this is so, is by way of a case study, so this is what we will do now.

Tulip Ltd and Crocus Ltd are two companies trading in the same industry. Their summarized trading and profit and loss accounts and working capital requirement for last year are shown in Figure 6.1.

Figure 6.1 Trading accounts of Tulip and Crocus (last year)

Trading and Profit & Loss Account	Tulip	Crocus
	£000	£000
Sales turnover	6,000	6,000
Cost of sales	4,200	4,200
Gross margin	1,800	1,800
Selling and administrative expenses	1,350	1,350
Operating profit	450	450
Bank interest	67	135
Net profit before tax	£383	£315

The bank overdraft interest for both companies is at the rate of 9 per cent per year, but Crocus pays twice the amount of interest because it runs its business with twice the amount of working capital. The working capital of the two companies, taken from their respective balance sheets, appears in Figure 6.2. For the sake of the computations in this example, it is supposed that the working capital – stocks plus debtors minus creditors – is funded by a bank overdraft in each company. So both companies make the same *operating* profit, but Crocus has less profit after interest, because it has to pay more interest on the higher bank overdraft it has.

Figure 6.2 Working capital figures for Tulip and Crocus

	Tulip	Crocus
Working capital	£000	£000
Stocks		
(A = 0.5 month of sales)	250	
(B = 1 month of sales)		500
Debtors		
(A = 2 months of sales)	1,000	
(B = 3 months of sales)		1,500
Creditors		
(A = Equivalent to 1 month of sales)	(500)	
(B = Same as A's creditors)		(500)
Working capital	£750	£1,500
Bank interest at 9% on overdraft facilities needed		
to fund working capital	£67	£135

EXERCISE

● ● ● ● ● ● ● ● ●

Is the fact that Crocus has twice the amount of working capital than its competitor, Tulip, any disadvantage? What are the longer-term implications of the lower net profit figure of Crocus?

Answer

It is important to note that both companies make the same *operating* profit (£450,000) and that the lower net profit of Crocus is because that company has a higher level of bank borrowing to finance its larger working capital. There is no other reason for the difference between the companies' net profit figures. So the main disadvantage of Crocus's higher level of working capital is the effect it has on Crocus's profitability. If the aim of business is to maximize the return on capital employed, as we have decided in Chapter 2, the higher level of working capital will *reduce* the numerator of the return on capital employed (profit) and *increase* the denominator (capital employed)! Capital employed will increase because it is represented by the total assets in the business, a constituent of which is the working capital.

The longer term implications of lower profit, if this were to happen year on year, would be that Crocus will have less profit to plough back into the business. What this means is that Crocus will grow slower than Tulip, because it has less money to invest in the business each year. Crocus's share price (if it were a quoted company) would rise slowly, whereas Tulip's would rise relatively quickly. Eventually, Tulip may be able to take over Crocus! This might be a good thing for Crocus's business – because Tulip might be able to control the working capital better than Crocus's management is!

There will be a long-term effect on Crocus because of the lower profit that it reports – and the company may be forced out of business just because it has too much money tied up in working capital. Another problem that Crocus will be faced with, however, is the impact that the higher working capital will have upon the cash flow of the company.

In order to demonstrate this, we will consider the cash position of each company a year later. Both companies' sales increased by 10 per cent during the year; 10 per cent more business is quite a lot to manage in one year, but let us assume for the sake of this example that it was possible to service such an increased level of business.

What would be the implications for the business you are in or for a business that you are familiar with of an increase of 10 per cent next year? Could the business cope with it? Would you require additional facilities? Additional staff? Additional working capital?

The need for additional working capital is illustrated below in the continuing story of Tulip and Crocus. Figure 6.3 shows that, following the 10 per cent increase in business, the sales turnover, cost of sales and therefore gross margin increased by 10 per cent. It is possible that selling and administrative expenses would not increase by the full 10 per cent, because some of the cost there would be fixed. If we assume that the expenses do increase by 10 per cent, the operating profit for both companies will also be 10 per cent more. So both companies make the same *operating* profit before interest is taken into account. On the other hand, as we shall see, the impact upon cash flow is quite dramatic.

Figure 6.3 Trading accounts of Tulip and Crocus (this year)

Trading and Profit & Loss Account		
	Tulip	Crocus
	£000	£000
Sales turnover	6,600	6,600
Cost of sales	4,620	4,620
Gross margin	1,980	1,980
Selling and administrative expenses	1,485	1,485
Operating profit	495	495
Bank interest (see below)	67	135
Net profit before tax	£428	£360

Note: Bank interest is taken to be at 9% of the bank overdraft at the beginning of the year, that is the same as last year's.

WORKOUT

EXERCISE

· · · · · · · · ·

What working capital figures would each company have after business increased by 10 per cent?

Answer

Figure 6.4 shows the amount of working capital of both companies following a 10 per cent rise in the level of business. Both companies have 10 per cent more working capital. There is 10 per cent more tied up in inventory because more stock is needed to meet the needs of the extra business. There are 10 per cent more debtors than last year, again because of the extra sales. Tulip's working capital has grown by £75,000. Crocus's working capital has grown by £150,000.

Figure 6.4   Working capital figures after growth of 10 percent in level of business

	Tulip £000	Crocus £000
Working capital		
Stocks		
(A = 0.5 month of sales)	275	
(B = 1 month of sales)		550
Debtors		
(A = 2 months of sales)	1,100	
(B = 3 months of sales)		1,650
Creditors		
(A = Equivalent to 1 month of sales)	(550)	
(B = Same as A's creditors)		(550)
Working capital	£825	£1,650

Both companies have to fund the extra working capital that they need. Where is the money to come from? It could come from the cash flow generated from operations, or each company could borrow more. If either company has to borrow more the impact will be twofold:

1. There will be an impact on profitability. More interest will have to be paid if more is borrowed and the profits available to the owners of the business will be lower.

2. There will be a need to arrange additional borrowing. Whether or not either company is able to raise the cash required to finance the extra working capital will depend upon the level of borrowing the company has already (and on the forecast ability to repay the borrowing!). But also, cash borrowed to fund working capital may reduce the amount that can be borrowed to invest in assets which will make a much more positive return to the shareholders.

The cash flow implications of taking on the extra 10 per cent of business are shown in Figure 6.5. We have made the following assumptions in order to calculate the cash flow implications of the extra 10 per cent of business for each company in our case study. We have assumed that:

★ Cash flow from operations is equal to the trading profit.

★ Depreciation has been charged as part of administrative expenses – and amounts to £200,000.

★ Both companies pay the interest on the bank overdraft at the beginning of the year – that is, the same interest as the year before.

★ Both companies pay a dividend of £250,000.

★ Both companies replace assets to the value of £220,000.

★ Both companies pay no tax.

Figure 6.5 The cash flow of Tulip and Crocus

Cash flow statement		
	Tulip	Crocus
	£000	£000
Cash flow from operations		
Trading profit after interest	495	495
Add Depreciation	200	200
Less Increased investment in working capital	(75)	(150)
	620	545
Dividends paid	(250)	(250)
Interest paid	(67)	(135)
Replacement of fixed assets investment	(220)	(220)
Net cash flow	£83	(£60)

You can see from Figure 6.5 that the cash flow for Tulip is positive (plus £83,000) whereas the cash flow for Crocus is negative (minus £60,000). Crocus will have to borrow more from the bank if it is to manage the extra business that has come its way. What are the reasons for this? The need for extra bank overdraft is because:

★ Crocus needs relatively more cash to finance its extra working capital. Crocus had to invest an extra £150,000 in working capital – while Tulip only needed to find £75,000.

★ Crocus is paying twice the amount of bank interest compared with Tulip, and that situation will worsen if Crocus borrows even more.

Tulip is able to meet the demand created from the extra business from its own cash resources. Crocus would have to borrow in order to finance the extra working capital required for the new business. Companies which do not control the amount tied up in working capital find it very difficult to grow without resort to a bank overdraft.

Better management of working capital – cash flow implications

Of course, Crocus could try to manage its working capital better. It has the benchmark of Tulip Ltd, a similar sized company in the same industry. There is little doubt that Crocus should be able to control its working capital to that of the level of Tulip Ltd. Crocus would have to pursue some of the policies and activities that Tulip endorses to improve its levels of stockholding and debtors. If Crocus could match the working capital levels of Tulip, the company could in fact generate £750,000 by releasing the working capital it has in excess of the amount that Tulip has. Crocus could use that to pay off some of the overdraft and thereby reduce the amount of interest paid to the bank. Crocus could then use any borrowing facilities thereby released to fund any further growth in its business.

Strategic implications of working capital management

Exactly how Tulip manages to keep its working capital under control, we shall deal with in the next section of this chapter. For the moment let us consider the strategic implications of such working capital control.

You may say that the effort to control working capital is short term and hardly has any strategic implications. That may be true because the cash saved is only saved once and the action required to reduce amounts tied up in working capital will be taken in the short run, say, over the next two years. However, there are two major strategic implications of the action that is taken to control the working capital:

★ First, the cash saved from improving the working capital can be used elsewhere in the business, to enable strategies to be achieved. Cash tied up in working capital cannot be said to be earning the company much return (in spite of it being called *working* capital!). It would be better to put the cash into fixed assets which can be used to produce goods and services rather than to let finances languish by funding working capital.

★ Second, there are implications in the way a business is perceived implied in tight working capital management. Companies which have low stocks and chase their debtors can arguably be said to be less customer friendly than those that hold large stocks (from which customers can readily select their goods) and who do not chase for their money after the sale is made. Such companies may attract a certain type of customer – one who expects a fair degree of service, but who does not expect to pay for such service!

Many customers today are much more sophisticated than the point just made suggests. Customers may prefer to deal with a tightly run ship which is obviously well managed; one which has its working capital under control and which is likely to be there in the future when they need you to supply them again. A company which has high stocks and high levels of debtors may be giving its customers a spuriously good level of service today but it may be so weighed down with excess working capital that it cannot compete and the business may not be able to afford to be there tomorrow.

So, strategically speaking, the day-to-day management of capital working is most important. Sound control of working capital allows cash flow generated from the profit of the business to be used for real growth. Retained earnings are used to buy assets which will generate even further growth, rather than increase the working capital. Furthermore, the company will be perceived by its customers as lean and efficient; someone with whom it is good to do business. What can be done to control the amount of working capital?

Stock control

So much has been written about stock management and so many systems have been developed that companies nowadays have just the right amount of stock – or know where to get it in time.

EXERCISE

WORKOUT

What do you understand by the term 'a just-in-time stock ordering system'?

Answer

A 'just-in-time stock ordering system' is one which ensures that raw materials or components or services required (very often for a production process) are available at the time they are required. The objective is for the producer to keep minimal stocks and to be able to draw down stocks from suppliers as and when required. This means that the user has to have a pretty good idea what the requirements are. In that way, the supplier can be advised what the likely call-off orders will be – in terms of amount and timing – daily, weekly, or monthly.

In terms of working capital management, manufacturers have the worst time of it; at any point in time they will have stocks of raw materials or components, stocks of part-finished products (work in progress) and stocks of finished goods. Retailers, on the other hand, have least stock, perhaps just one or two items in stock for each product line for the customer to peruse. On-line centralized ordering systems ensure that the retailer is 'topped up' urgently if a customer takes the last item in stock. Sometimes the customer has to wait. The next exercise asks you to think of situations when that is acceptable.

EXERCISE

· · · · · · · · ·

WORKOUT

Can you think of examples where the customer is willing to wait for goods or services?

Answer

There are examples where the customer has to wait and is willing to wait. Here are a few that I have thought of, no doubt you can think of others.

★ Furniture stores often order items for you which take several weeks to deliver – especially if you choose a particular fabric associated with a specific design of a piece of furniture.

★ Car dealerships rarely have the precise model of a new car that you want in their showrooms. They will demonstrate using a typical model but when you order a specific model, engine size, colour and so on, they will 'find' one for you through a centralized computer system. If one is not available elsewhere in stock, an order will prompt the manufacturer and the car of your choice will be manufactured.

★ Goods made to order or customer's specification.

★ Building contracts.

You might think that businesses which provide a service do not hold stock, so stockholding is not a problem to them. The next exercise asks you to question this assertion.

EXERCISE

Do service providers have stock? For example, do banks have any stock that they need to control? Do software consultants who design specialist software to order have stock?

Answer

Banks do not have any stock as such but they do hold a certain amount of cash of course! The amount of cash they hold is regulated by government authorities rather than the determination by the banks to hold a certain level of liquidity. To banks, holding cash has an opportunity cost, because the cash is not earning interest, so they do not like to hold more than they have to.

Many service providers have stock – or work in progress – where the contract is to deliver a service over a period of time. Milestones during the contract may be agreed and payments may be made by the customer or client, but inevitably there is a lot of time and cost tied up in the contract at any particular time. This has to be financed.

Stock control techniques

It may sound very trite to say it but if only a business knew what it was going to sell it could always make sure it had the right goods or services available at the time that they were required! So how do businesses ensure that they have the minimal, but yet enough stock? It is all down to sales forecasting. But as we all know, this is extremely difficult to do. So business has resorted to the analysis of the likely demand to stock and order processing systems which ensure that stock is available or that it can be obtained very quickly. This may involve just-in-time systems and certainly sound relations with suppliers, with whom there has to be an almost joint venture relationship these days.

Control of debtors

Collecting money from customers is one of the chores of business that no doubt we could all do without. If only customers would pay on time.

The most often used period of credit – 30 days – usually extends to an average of 45 days because effectively any goods purchased this month are paid for at the end of next month. This averages out to a period of 45 debtors' days. If payment slides into the month following, the debtors' days creep up to an average of 60 days or more, although only 30 days' credit was given technically.

Part of the reason for this, of course, is that our accounting systems tend to work on a monthly cycle. So all the invoices from a particular supplier are collected together and processed during the month following. By the time the processing of the invoices has taken place – invoices checked to delivery notes to ensure that the goods have been received, invoices posted to accounting ledgers and authorization of payment made – the end of the month following has been reached. This rather weak reason for paying late is provided as an explanation rather than an excuse for paying late. Certainly it is unlikely that where many invoices are received from a supplier that they will be paid individually after 30 days. It seems sensible to accumulate invoices and make one payment.

The main reason for lengthening the actual credit periods taken is that, of course, cash in my bank is better for me than cash in your bank. This is because if I have the cash I can spend it or, at least, earn interest on it. I am better off. But there are two sides to this issue. The other is that if a business is to have the close relationship with its suppliers that was suggested above, it is important to pay them on time.

So what can be done? What procedures and tools do we have in financial management to help us manage the debtors' days best? There are a number of headings under which this issue can be explored.

1. Credit control departments.

2. Offering discounts for early payment.

3. Charging penalty interest.

4. Factoring and invoice discounting.

Credit control departments

Any business that is selling goods on credit will have to have some form of credit control department. A credit controller will ensure that checks are made upon the balances owing by specific customers. Any amounts overdue will be pursued by collecting methods ranging from reminders – for example, statements of outstanding balances – to chasing telephone calls, to pursuing payment through the law courts. Sound financial management of this kind that keeps right on top of customers' accounts will pay big dividends over time. If debtors are allowed to take longer terms of credit over a period of time it is very difficult to bring them back into line.

> *If debtors are allowed to take longer terms of credit over a period of time it is very difficult to bring them back into line.*

Discounts for early payment

The terms on which a company trades its supplies and services, if it is to offer a discount for early payment, are typically referred to as 30 days, less 2 per cent for payment in ten days. This means that the customer can deduct 2 per cent from its bills if it pays them within ten days of receiving them, although the payment in full is due in 30 days. Though 2 per cent may not sound like very much, the company is giving up 2 per cent of revenue just for the privilege of receiving its cash from customers 20 days earlier than it would have done otherwise. The effective cost of this can be expressed as an annual percentage rate, calculated as follows: 20 days is approximately one-eighteenth of one year, so the annual rate is 2 per cent times 18, or 36 per cent.

Note: The annualized cost of offering an early settlement discount can be found by using the following formula:

$$\frac{\% \text{ Cash discount}}{100\% - \% \text{ Cash discount}} \times \frac{365 \text{ days}}{\text{Date for net payment} - \text{Date for discount payment}}$$

EXERCISE

Calculate the annual percentage cost of offering a 1½ per cent discount for payment on delivery (nil credit days) rather than in 30 days.

Answer

The annual percentage is:

$$\frac{1\frac{1}{2}\%}{100\% - 1\frac{1}{2}\%} \times \frac{365 \text{ days}}{30 - 0}$$

$$= \frac{0.015}{0.985} \times \frac{365}{30}$$

$$= 0.185 \text{ (or } 18.5\%)$$

The cost of receiving the cash from customers' accounts 20 days earlier than otherwise is effectively an annual interest rate of 36 per cent. This is pretty expensive finance. Only if the company can use the cash to earn a better return than 36 per cent, should it offer such a generous discount for early settlement. We must now ask, therefore, whether it is worthwhile for a company to offer early payment discount terms to its customers. The answer is that it depends on the opportunity cost of the funds that would otherwise have been locked up in debtors, and whether it justifies the reduction in net sales revenues. Where the effective cost of offering the discount is 36 per cent, it may be difficult to find investment which will offer that sort of return. But if the early settlement discount rate is lower, the decision may be closer, as the following example shows.

Assume that a company's terms of trade are 30 days and that just 1 per cent discount is offered for payment received within ten days. This represents an annual percentage cost of 18 per cent (one-eighteenth of a year times 1 per cent). If 25 per cent of its customers actually take advantage of this discount and annual sales are £12 million, customers involved in £3 million of revenue will take the discount. The discount cost is, therefore, 1 per cent of £3 million, or £30,000.

Assuming that 25 per cent of the customers pay in ten days and the rest pay in 30, the average collection period, including both discount and non-discount sales, is 25 days ($0.75 \times 30 + 0.25 \times 10$), giving average debtors in this case of approximately £820,000, as shown in the following equation:

$$\frac{£12,000,000 \times 25}{365} = £821,918$$

If the company did not give a discount, none of its customers would pay within ten days and the average collection period would fall from 25 to 30 days. In that case, average debtors would be £986,300.

$$\frac{£12,000,000 \times 30}{365} = £986,300$$

The question is, then, what return the company can make on approximately £166,000, the amount by which the discount policy has reduced the average debtors. If the return on the investment of £166,000 exceeds the £30,000 cost of the discount policy – which is, of course, approximately 18 per cent – then the policy will be worthwhile. It is quite possible for the company to make a return on investment elsewhere in the business of 18 per cent. Although it may be difficult to find investment with returns higher than 18 per cent, the company may very well wish to use this source of cash – early payment by customers – to finance growth elsewhere, rather than raising funds outside the company.

Penalty interest

It is conventional in certain businesses – for example, in commodity trading – to charge interest on overdue credit balances. The original contract for sale will state that, for example, 2½ per cent per month interest will be added to any late payments of credit accounts. As was explained in the previous paragraph, the cost of this can be very high as a percentage rate. Although the system of penalty interest does work in some businesses, it is fair to say that for many businesses the accounting procedures are not available to calculate precisely the amount of interest that should be charged on overdue accounts. Where many invoices are involved each month covering many different dates the calculations involved would mean an addition to the accounting software that most companies have at their disposal. Again, this is not an excuse but a reason why many companies do not charge or attempt to charge penalty interest.

Factoring and invoice discounting

Some companies have chosen to assign or actually sell their debtors to another firm; a financial institution or finance company. In such arrangements – known as *factoring* or *invoice discounting* – the operating company effectively borrows cash from the financial institution against the invoices sent to its customers.

1. *Factoring* means that the finance company or bank provides cash advances up to an agreed percentage of each invoice for a fee. They then collect the remittances directly from the customers. It is probably most relevant for small, but growing, companies with less than £25 million annual sales.

2. *Invoice discounting* is purely a financial arrangement which converts invoices into cash through specialized finance companies. The trading company is responsible for collecting the debt and for repaying the amount advanced, whether the debt is collected or not.

Factoring is more a means of financing the business than it is a means of collecting accounts when due from customers. For this reason it is really a strategic decision to decide upon factoring or invoice discounting rather than to raise the funds to finance debtors from the company's own resources. On the other hand it might be possible to factor debts rather than to finance them with an overdraft facility. This is because the banks are happy to provide finance for sales which have already been made rather than to lend to the company on the basis of a general overdraft facility. Finance offered by way of factoring means that the current lending outstanding is associated with the volume of business directly. As the business increases so too does the financing: as business falls away the amount of finance involved will reduce. In this way the bank lending on this basis will not have to monitor the lending quite as closely. If they offer finance by way of a bank overdraft that facility has to be reviewed at regular intervals by the bank, with a concurrent cost of doing that. So the banks like factoring or invoice discounting and their customers may be happy with it because the amount of finance is associated with the volume of business. If the business grows, then so too does the amount of finance and the business does not have to apply to the bank to extend its overdraft facilities.

Control of creditors' balances (accounts payable)

The effect of minimal stock holding and slow payment of accounts by customers is, of course, that the working capital problem is passed on to the supplier. Many companies who pay their supplier slowly *and* expect them to hold stocks for them – so that they are available when required – may not consider the effect all this might have on their suppliers. At the very least, resentment will build up between the supplier and customer and relationships, which ideally need to have a sense of common purpose, will sour. The supplier may become less and less willing to supply to a late payer and will not give the best service to that customer. Priority will be given to those who pay on time. If the worst comes to the worst, the supplier may be forced out of business if his or her cash flow becomes very sluggish because of late payers. The supplier will not be able to pay his or her suppliers and employees.

We can conclude that any business is ill advised to squeeze its suppliers by paying them late, even though the cash in the bank is better there than in its suppliers'. Although trade credit is apparently a source of finance, we would argue that it should be used very sparingly as a means of financing the business over the longer term. This does not mean that companies should not take the period of credit offered by the suppliers, because the supplier has budgeted for that term of payment in his financial management and pricing policy. But if that period of credit is extended then one cannot expect to be in receipt of the same level of service from the supplier.

Cash management

This chapter so far has emphasized the need to control the assets used in the business because for every pound or dollar that is required to run the business, the same amount of money has to be found to finance those assets. But another major aspect of assets, and of working capital in particular, is its effect on cash flow. The effect of sound asset management from the cash point of view is more dynamic than seeking to find the amount of finance that is needed to fund the acquisition of the assets at any particular moment in time. Cash management involves cash flow forecasting over a period of time rather than at a point in time. Cash management is such an important issue from the strategic point of view that we dedicate a whole chapter in this Workout to the management of cash in the business. Chapter 7 explains why cash is such an important resource and how it needs to be carefully controlled.

Review of management of working capital

Much of what we have been discussing may not appear to have any strategic implication. The control of stocks and debtors and even the replacement of plant and machinery when required may simply appear to have implications only for short-term financial management. But I believe in each case there are strategic decisions and assumptions to be made in the management of assets. For example:

★ Most companies these days attempt to minimize stock levels. But it is a strategic decision to choose to expect suppliers to hold stocks that are needed in production and supply them when required just in time. Exactly what does the relationship have to be in order that a business is willing to rely on another in this way?

★ There are certainly strategic marketing implications as to the length of credit given to customers and whether or not they are pressed to pay on time. However, it has to be said that we all expect to be chased for payment of late accounts these days, so it is unlikely that any goodwill will be lost by reminding customers that they owe you an overdue account. Indeed, they may regard you more highly if they are pressed for payment – they may regard you as a more efficient organization – than if you leave the account unpaid and do not remind your customer.

Part Three

LONG-TERM FITNESS

• • • • •

Financial appraisal techniques in the longer term

How to use Part Three

This part of the Workout sets out the financial procedures that have to be used when making investment in the longer term; when capital investment is made in the business.

★ Use it to gauge the adequacy of the cash flows in your business. Seek to evaluate the need for new finance and to assess the investments into which the new funds are placed.

★ Review the position of your business in terms of the risks it faces and how such risks are measured.

Managing cash

WORKOUT

1 Why is it important to measure the cash flow as well as the profit of a business?

2 For what reasons does cash flow differ from profit?

3 Do expanding businesses need more cash or less cash?

4 What is the difference between a cash flow forecast and a budgeted cash flow statement?

5 What alternative policies are there if the cash flow forecasts over the longer term indicate that there is a deficit in the cash flows expected?

Adequacy of cash flow

The importance of cash flow to a business has been likened to the blood supply in the human body. While it is important that you have enough blood, it is just as important that it is flowing through the body and reaching the parts that matter. So it is with cash flow in the business: it is not solely the amount of cash that the business has but whether there is adequate cash *flow*. In fact cash can be called the lifeblood of a business. Cash keeps the business going. It is the mechanism through which most business is carried out.

Companies have to have someone who keeps an eye on the cash, so that it does not run out. That person has to forecast the cash flow, probably on a daily basis, so that cash is available when payments have to be made. This is just as it is with your own personal financial affairs. Someone in your household has to estimate the cash outgoings and compare them with your income otherwise you do not 'manage'.

The management of cash

It is so easy to tie up cash in the business. You may have heard your managing director or your financial accountant saying: 'We are making enough profit, but we never see any of the cash that should be generated by such a successful business.' The irony is that this is often the case: successful businesses are often short of cash because investment is being made in the business. An unprofitable business may well generate cash for a while. This is because stocks are running down, customers' debtors' balances are falling and assets are not being replaced. The unprofitable business may also be selling off parts of the business, which generates cash, of course.

Expanding businesses – those that are doing very well – will usually be short of funds during the period of their growth. We saw in Chapters 5 and 6 how important it was to keep a tight control on both fixed and current assets in order to achieve a good return on capital employed. For cash management, too, it is sound financial management to keep control of the amount invested in assets. Cash invested in assets has to be raised by borrowing or by asking the shareholders for more equity. Some will come from the profits of the business, provided those profits can be turned into cash. As so often happens, however, cash becomes tied up in the working capital or it is spent on buying new assets for the business. This is so easy to do when the cash is available, when the business is profitable, and when there is no pressure on cash resources.

> *Expanding businesses – those that are doing very well – will usually be short of funds during the period of their growth.*

Cash flow forecasting

Careful control of the cash required for investment and for working capital will enable the business to grow, using its own resources rather than having to borrow in order to expand the business. So that cash is available for the payments that a company has to make as routine, as well as those that are made less often, a cash flow forecast has to be prepared. This will give some idea whether or not the company can 'pay its way'.

The elements of the cash flow forecast can be separated into three categories:

1. Receipts from sales activity. The amount and timing of receipts from debtors' accounts has to be predicted.

2. Routine payments. Routine payments are made for supplies and expenses on a regular basis – perhaps monthly or weekly – in any business. The timing and the amount of routine payments have to be predicted:

    –   for payments to suppliers for goods and services supplied

    –   for payments made to, and on behalf of, employees such as salaries, taxes, social security, travelling costs, welfare and corporate pensions contributions

    –   for expenses such as rent, utilities and telephones and communications costs.

3. Non-routine payments. There will be major items of single, one-off payments during the year such as:

    –   the purchase of fixed assets

    –   large unusual cash expenditures on such items as sales promotions, R&D projects and large training programmes

    –   dividends paid to shareholders

    –   interest paid to lenders

    –   taxation payments.

The effect of the non-routine, irregular payments is that a 'lumpy' cash flow profile is created. Sometimes there will be positive cash flow; at others there will be a negative cash flow. Managing this uneven process requires some skill and a need to keep cash balances and forecasts under constant review. And that constant review means *daily*. Someone in every business has to have what might be called a corporate treasury role to check daily on the bank balance(s). This is in order to make sure that there are enough funds to make the payments required on any particular day. For example, it may be the day to pay salaries, or it may be the day to pay a major supplier. The funds have to be there. If they are not, there may be serious implications. There probably will be if salaries are not paid on time! So, someone has to look after this short-run cash flow forecast of immediate cash needs and expected receipts in the near future.

But what about the longer-term trends? What about having the cash available for the larger, irregular payments; for dividends to be paid to shareholders, for corporate taxes and so on? How can we be sure that the funds will be available for those payments?

EXECUTIVE
ACTION

Consider your own personal household budget. How do you make sure that there is enough in your family bank account to pay those bills that are always coming in? How do you save up for the larger, single annual payments, like the annual family vacation?

CASE STUDY

To demonstrate the use of the cash flow forecast we shall take the example of a fictitious building contractor, Commercial Contractors plc, a construction company which, for the most part, contracts to build commercial properties in the centre of large cities. Initially, we shall look into the cash flow forecast of a division of Commercial Contractors, Liverpool City Construction (LCC). Later, we shall consider the cash flow management of Commercial Contractors overall, at corporate level. It is important to see, however, that the corporate cash flow is a function of all the individual business units' cash flows.

The cash flow forecast

Managers at LCC are allowed a working bank balance of £100,000. If the bank balance goes below zero, the amount has to be borrowed from Commercial Contractors' corporate treasury at 10 per cent per year interest. So it is well worthwhile the managers of LCC planning their cash flow very carefully so that their profits do not have to take the 'hit' of an interest charge, something which was probably not allowed for in their budget. They will require their management accountant to prepare at least a monthly cash flow forecast. In practice, a weekly cash flow forecast will be prepared (or even more frequently than that). Certainly someone has to keep a constant eye on the cash flow and make regular forecasts.

LCC have relatively few building projects but each is of high value. Sales receipts are in the nature of contract payments on account, as certain milestones, set out in each contract, are reached. The trouble with this is that the total of receipts is an irregular amount and it is quite possible that the business will have to borrow from the corporate treasury at certain times, particularly when they are awaiting payments on a large contract. Frank Wiles, LCC's management accountant, estimates that the sales receipts for the first six months of 1997, based on the budget, but taking into account the expected timing of receipts, will be:

	£000
January	970
February	1,912
March	2,998
April	1,075
May	2,310
June	2,544

Assuming that LCC prepare only a monthly cash flow forecast, those estimated cash receipts for each month will be inserted into the forecast as shown in Figure 7.1.

If we are provided with all the payments that are expected to be made over the same six months in each of the cost categories included in the budget, we will be able to see whether or not LCC will need to resort to borrowing from corporate treasury. The exercise on the next page asks you to complete the cash flow forecast started in Figure 7.1.

Figure 7.1   LCC's cash flow forecast

	Jan £000	Feb £000	Mar £000	Apr £000	May £000	June £000
Opening balance	100					
Sales receipts	970	1,912	2,998	1,075	2,310	2,544

Payments
  Wages and salaries
  Personnel costs
  Payments to sub-contractors
  Equipment hire and running costs
  Office and administration costs
  Payment on leased assets
  Head office allocation						

Total payments						
Interest (10% per year on previous month's closing balance)						
Closing balance						

WORKOUT

EXERCISE

Complete Figure 7.1. Assume that the cash payments for LCC's cash flow forecast over the next six months are those shown in Figure 7.2. The forecast cash receipts discussed above are already included in Figure 7.1. Remember interest is charged at 10 per cent per year on negative cash balances. It is not 'received' on positive cash balances. The interest paid is based on any negative bank balance at the end of the previous month.

Is there any action that the local management of LCC can take to improve their cash flow?

Figure 7.2   LCC's payments forecast for January to June

	Jan £000	Feb £000	Mar £000	Apr £000	May £000	June £000
Wages and salaries	810	810	858	820	823	865
Personnel costs – travelling, training, etc	70	101	68	113	153	92
Payments to sub-contractors	154	1,478	488	693	899	994
Equipment hire and running costs	48	33	23	19	58	68
Office and administration costs	254	254	276	289	254	263
Payment on leased assets	30	30	30	30	30	30
Head office allocation – paid in cash	126	126	126	126	126	126

Answer

LCC's complete cash flow forecast for the six months appears in Figure 7.3.

Figure 7.3   LCC's completed cash flow forecast

	Jan £000	Feb £000	Mar £000	Apr £000	May £000	June £000
Opening balance	100	(422)	(1,346)	(228)	(1,245)	(1,288)
Sales receipts	970	1,912	2,998	1,075	2,310	2,544
Payments						
Wages and salaries	810	810	858	820	823	865
Personnel costs	70	101	68	113	153	92
Payments to sub-contractors	154	1,478	488	693	899	994
Equipment hire and running costs	48	33	23	19	58	68
Office and administration costs	254	254	276	289	254	263
Payment on leased assets	30	30	30	30	30	30
Head office allocation	126	126	126	126	126	126
Total payments	1,492	2,832	1,869	2,090	2,343	2,438
Interest (10% per year on previous month's balance)	–	4	11	2	10	11
Closing balance	(422)	(1,346)	(228)	(1,245)	(1,288)	(1,193)

Comment on LCC's cash flow forecast

Could LCC 'improve' the cash flow that was forecast? LCC need to borrow throughout, particularly in February, April, May and June when the borrowing requirement is over £1 million. The large payment to sub-contractors in February – and the low receipts expected in January – cause particular problems.

In order to reduce, or even avoid, such a deficit, LCC could:

(a) try to accelerate receipts on contracts

(b) delay making payments to suppliers for some weeks

(c) make some cost cuts, although this may take time to work through to the cash budget.

Corporate control of cash

The object of the cash flow forecast is to make sure as far as it is possible that cash is available to make payments when they become due for such things as salaries and payments to suppliers. Each business unit will be expected to keep within its forecast cash requirements, or, at least, give as much notice of any expected variation as possible. Business units will be expected therefore not only to generate revenue but also to ensure that receipts from it are forthcoming on time. They will be expected to keep within cost budgets, not just because of maintaining profitability (which is most important) but because costs have to be paid for. Costs which are out of control will have adverse cash flow implications too. In fact each business unit will be expected to manage its working capital in the ways we discussed in Chapter 6.

EXECUTIVE
ACTION

Many organizations only pay the commissions or bonuses of their sales people after the cash has been received from customers. Is this the way it works in your organization? Do you involve sales people in collecting balances due from customers, or do you have a credit control department which does that? Consider the advantages and disadvantages of asking sales people to become involved in collecting receivables.

A longer-term, underlying trend, however, may develop from the cash flow profile. For example, as we saw in Chapter 6, an expanding business will require cash injections to fund working capital growth. Furthermore, an expanding business will usually require investment in additional fixed assets to enable it to handle extra business. In this way strategic questions will arise from cash flow planning. There may be, from time to time, the need for major injections of cash and the need for longer-term finance. Such situations will probably only be noticed at corporate level where the whole cash flow picture can be seen. The corporate cash flow forecast will suggest whether or not the business as a whole needs to raise more capital.

Returning to the Commercial Contractors case study, the group consists of ten divisions in several countries in Europe. Each division would provide Commercial Contractors, at corporate level, with a similar cash flow forecast to that of LCC. Each division might be making large payments for some reason in February. They might be acquiring new equipment for building sites, more scaffolding for example, or they might be indulging in a large advertising and promotional campaign in their local area. If cash flow forecasts for the ten divisions all showed around a £1.3 million cash requirement in February, the company, as a whole, would have to find funds amounting to over £13 million! LCC needs to borrow just over £1.3 million, so ten divisions would need to borrow over £13 million by the end of February. Commercial Contractors would have to have access to that amount of funds, otherwise they will not be able to make some payments in February.

The need to raise £13 million is, of course, a forecast requirement. The essence of the cash flow forecast is that Commercial Contractors know that they are likely to require around £13 million by the end of February. Something can be done about it now rather than waiting until February and finding out that they have a cash flow crisis.

Whether the company uses short-term bank overdraft facilities – and this would be a question of persuading its bankers to lend that amount of money in the short term – or whether longer-term funds are needed, would depend upon forecasting for a longer period than six months. The problem is that the further ahead the company looks the more difficult it is to say, with any degree of accuracy, exactly what the cash requirements are. Longer-term cash flow forecasting tends to be uncertain. What this means is that there is less accuracy in the figures. The future is hard to predict accurately, and exactly when cash is to be received and spent is difficult to forecast precisely.

New finance

A longer-term cash flow forecast might throw up the need for additional permanent finance. A company which is growing rapidly might need all of the cash flow generated from the profits of the business for working capital requirements. Cash required for large capital expenditures, large research and development programmes or large sales and promotion campaigns, will have to be raised by issuing more shares on the stock exchange or by borrowing from banks or other lending institutions. The company will know it has to raise funds in the market, if these do not seem to be forthcoming from the surplus cash flow from trading over the years.

Companies planning their financing requirements will need to produce a *budgeted cash flow statement*. A budgeted cash flow statement or budgeted funds statement looks at the total cash flow requirements of the business over the year or years ahead. In this instance, we are not so much interested in predicting *when* particular payments are to be made or receipts are to be expected, which is the intention of the cash flow forecast. The cash flow forecast aims at establishing whether there is a need for funds at a particular point in time so that a particular payment can be made. The intention of the budgeted cash flow statement is to predict the overall cash flow requirements in terms of the adequacy of the level of finance available.

> **A longer-term cash flow forecast might throw up the need for additional permanent finance.**

An example of the budgeted cash flow statement

We continue to use the example of Commercial Contractors. At corporate level, the company might plan its cash flow over the next five years. This would be the shortest period over which to judge the longer-term cash resources requirement of the company. Figure 7.4 shows what the accountants feel are the cash flow implications of the future plans of Commercial Contractors for the next five years.

Remember that the budgeted cash flow statement uses the figures for the group as a whole, rather than those of any one division. Assuming that Commercial Contractors had the ten divisions suggested earlier, in February 1997 it was suggested that the cash requirement could have been £13 million. By the *end* of 1997, the budgeted cash flow in Figure 7.4 shows that the requirements for funding for the whole group was expected to be as much as £25 million.

The plans for the years after that indicate that the company more or less expects to break even in terms of cash flow. There is not a large surplus of funds nor a large deficit of funds in the years 1998–2001. There is, thus, no expectation that any repayment of the £25 million required by the end of 1997 will be possible in the following four years. As there appears to be no possibility of repaying the £25 million, it seems that longer-term capital is required.

Figure 7.4   Commercial Contractors' budgeted cash flow statement for five years

	1997 £m	1998 £m	1999 £m	2000 £m	2001 £m
Opening balance	2.3	(24.9)	(25.1)	(25.0)	(24.9)
Sales receipts	177.4	199.8	197.6	201.0	201.0
Payments					
Business running costs	142.6	152.2	149.1	150.0	150.0
Interest payments	9.3	11.4	11.4	11.4	11.4
Tax payments	15.9	16.8	16.9	17.1	17.1
Dividends paid	16.1	16.7	17.3	18.0	18.0
Capital investment in the business	20.7	2.9	2.8	4.4	4.4
Total payments	204.6	200.0	197.5	200.9	200.9
Closing balance	(24.9)	(25.1)	(25.0)	(24.9)	(24.8)

EXERCISE

• • • • • • • • •

Once again, it is instructive to ask you to review the budgeted cash flow statement in Figure 7.4. What do you feel are the main causes of the need for additional funds in 1997? Do you consider that Commercial Contractors have any alternative policy, other than raising additional funds to finance the business.

Answer

The cash flow deficit in 1997 appears to be mainly the result of the anticipated low sales receipts figure in that year. There may be a number of reasons for this: less business generally or business taken on at lower margins (lower sales prices). In a competitive climate there may be little that Commercial Contractors' management can do about this situation. It may be possible to trim costs, but most contractors would take the view that it is better to make sales (and thereby cover some of their fixed costs) than not to make them at all.

Whether or not Commercial Contractors should raise more finance would depend upon the company's profitability. As far as can be judged from the cash flow evidence, the company could be making a loss in 1997, and very little profit in the years 1998–2001.

The budgeted cash flow statement may indicate that there is a requirement for long-term capital. Consequently, longer-term capital should be sought. Broadly, the choice is between borrowing the funds required, on the one hand, and raising more funds from the shareholders, on the other. Long-term debt – repayable, say, over five to ten years – could be arranged. Alternatively, additional shares could be issued to the company's shareholders. The choice between debt (long-term borrowing) and equity (shareholder funds) is discussed in the next chapter.

Conclusion

As the operations of a company go on day by day and month by month, they cause cash to be received and cash to be paid out. These receipts and payments will rarely match each other. Also, large cash outflows will occur at times; such as when taxes or a major new capital investment have to be paid for. So the cash balances of a company at any point in time can be either in surplus or in deficit.

There are two reasons for planning cash flows. The first is to ensure that any short-term shortages of funds that are predicted, can be met by having funds available when required. This means that overdraft facilities or other short-term loans should be negotiated and arranged well in advance of having to use them. It is much easier to negotiate a short-term loan *in advance* rather than attempt to secure funds at the last minute in a crisis. Producing cash flow forecasts – even if they show cash deficits – gives an indication of good management, even though the managers may be running short of cash!

The second reason for planning cash flow is longer term. The business may just realize that there is constant pressure on cash flow, that short-term funds are always being required. In this situation the business may simply be short of enough finance with which to run the business; it is what is called 'under funded'. In this case the cash flow forecast will point to the need to raise more funds. We turn, in the next chapter, to look at exactly how companies decide how much they should raise as long-term finance. We consider whether they should issue more shares to their shareholders or whether they should borrow more from their bank or from various other institutional lenders that are in the financial markets.

Strategic plans and finance

How do you link the need for long-term
funds with a company's strategy?

· · · · · · · · · ·

Raising finance

· · · · · · · · · ·

'Selling' the financial plans to the market

· · · · · · · · · ·

Debt versus equity

· · · · · · · · · ·

Why the current state of the financial
markets is important

· · · · · · · · · ·

The importance of financial gearing
or leverage

· · · · · · · · · ·

The cost of debt and equity

The need for new finance

We saw in Chapter 1 that companies will plan for three to five years ahead in some detail, will plan further ahead than that in less detail, and will aim for those plans to meet certain financial objectives. In the chapters which followed we saw that the business also has to assess where it is now and what it has to do – what decisions it has to take – in order to achieve those strategies. These strategies that may well involve expansion. Fixed assets will be required to manufacture the products or to deliver the service, and working capital may be required to support the extra sales. This expenditure will need financing.

The main source of funds for any business on an on-going basis will be the cash resulting from profits. Cash flow arises from profits because the company aims to provide goods and services at prices which are greater than the costs, so that receipts are higher than cash paid out to meet the costs. Cash flow forecasts will be prepared, as we saw in Chapter 7, to see whether, in the short run, there is a need for cash, just in case the expected receipts do not match the payments. At corporate level, budgeted cash flow statements will be

> *The main source of funds for any business on an on-going basis will be the cash resulting from profits.*

prepared to see whether there is a need for finance in the longer run. If these indicate that the business is short of long-term funds, extra finance will be needed. In this chapter we consider how those funds might be raised.

Raising finance

Strategic plans will tend to take businesses into new fields. This will mean raising new capital, rather than simply relying on better management of current cash resources. That policy is of benefit in the short term – for example to prevent short-term bank borrowing – but it will be aggravating in the longer term if the company seems permanently short of cash, always on the edge of a cash flow crisis and not able to take up obviously profitable investment proposals when the opportunity arises.

Strategic decisions will take a business into new markets, with new products and using new technologies. Such decisions are usually taken at corporate level although there is no reason why a business unit should not change its strategy. But, for the most part, new strategic activities are put in place by corporate management into new business units.

One of the reasons for this is that the cash flow from one business in a group may be sufficient to fund another business unit. In this way, the group may avoid having to raise funds by borrowing or from its shareholders.

The awareness of a need for new funding will be observed at corporate level from its budgeted funds statement. This is usually how the demand for funds arises. Strategic planning will ideally be undertaken so that the cash required will be available as and when it is required. The forward plans of a company will be expressed in terms of sales revenue and profits and returns on capital employed, but it will also be necessary to convert the plans to budget for the anticipated cash flow.

Some plans will be so expansionary that there will be a cash flow shortage. In this case, funds will have to be raised either for the short term or for the medium term or even for the longer term. If the cash flow deficits forecast are only to be short-lived then short-term borrowing will suffice. This means taking up bank overdraft facilities or short-term bank loans which will be repaid when the rate of expansion levels off. Figure 8.1 shows a simplified example of this where a company borrows

Figure 8.1 Repayment of a bank loan

	Year 1 £000	Year 2 £000	Year 3 £000
Opening balance	200	53	5
Sales receipts	1,000	1,200	1,400
Total payments (including interest)	(880)	(981)	(1,031)
Loan repayments	(267)	(267)	(267)
Closing balance	53	5	107

£800,000 from the bank and this is repaid from cash flows generated by the business over the next three years.

The need for longer-term capital

If the apparent cash flow shortage indicated by the budgeted funds statement is long term, there may be no possibility that the capital will be repaid. In that case permanent capital will be needed. This means that long-term loans or additional share capital will be required. We shall explain below the factors which help corporate treasurers decide whether to raise debt or equity.

Generally, the short-term cash flow forecast is linked to a longer-term forecast. Many firms prepare a long-term forecast of three to five years, some much longer term than that. Long-term plans include estimating the size of the need for funds for long-term expansion, following expectations of growth and necessary capital investment related to such growth. Obviously, a long-term forecast of five years or more is subject to errors resulting from unanticipated events. The long-term forecast, however, does provide targets for the level of cash required in the business, and management can strive to achieve these. The plans can be updated as new information becomes available.

Selling the strategic plans to the market

If we have determined that there is a genuine need for long-term finance, then the next step in the process to raise funds is to establish the 'story' that is going to be told to the market. In the case of Commercial Contractors, their merchant bankers and stockbrokers will help them to put together a package which is attractive either to shareholders or to lenders.

Much will depend upon the future plans of Commercial Contractors and exactly how these may be hyped. The problem is that companies do not wish to give too much away to their competitors. If Commercial Contractors, for example, wanted to acquire another company, the prospectus for new capital would almost certainly not say anything about Commercial Contractors wanting to buy such and such a company. It would simply say that the funds were needed for acquisitions. So most prospectuses are written in general terms rather than stating what the actual funds are required for. Having said that a good deal of detailed information will be provided.

EXERCISE

WORKOUT

The case study which follows provides an example of a company raising funds in the market. Before you work your way through it you may like to consider when it would be a good time to borrow funds – that is, increase the level of debt the company has – or to raise more equity – that is, ask the shareholders to increase their investment in the company.

Answer

It is probably best to set the answer to this exercise in the context of a particular economic setting. You really want to know the state of the stock market, the level of interest rates and so on before you can answer this question. It is a practical problem rather than an academic issue. There is no suggested answer, therefore, to the above activity because so much depends on the economic and business environment at the time that the raising of funds is considered. All the points the exercise raises, however, are dealt with in the practical context of the case study below.

CASE STUDY

The principal activities of Pahshok plc, a company based in the UK, are food processing and distribution. The company specializes in the processing of vegetables from its own farms throughout the world and in the production of prepared meals for the catering trade. The company also has a large share of the market for the importation and distribution of fresh fruit and vegetables.

The company has grown steadily over the last five years, and has relied increasingly on bank overdraft facilities. Pahshok requires funds for three reasons.

1. To finance its continued expansion.

2. To replace plant and equipment.

3. To reduce the bank overdraft.

Consequently, the company is proposing to make a rights issue to its present shareholders on the basis of five new shares at 425p for every 100 shares held. The public reason for the rights issue will be that the funds are required for 'expansion and possible acquisition'.

Figure 8.2 lists certain current financial information about Pahshok and Figure 8.3 shows Pahshok's balance sheet at 31 December 1996.

Figure 8.2 Historical information about Pahshok plc

Total sales for the year to 31 December 1996 were £187 million.

Profits before tax (after charging loan stock interest) for the last five years are:

Year ended 31 December:	£m
1992	12.3
1993	13.6
1994	15.0
1995	16.9
1996	16.2

Corporate taxation is payable on these profits at the rate of 33 per cent nine months in arrears. Consequently, the corporate tax payable on the profits for the year to December 1996 of £5.3 million (33 per cent of £16.2 million) is payable on 1 October 1997.

The balance sheet of Pahshok as at 31 December 1996 is shown in Figure 8.3.

The proposed final dividend is 9p (an interim dividend of 6p having already been paid) and the current market price of the shares is 425p.

The present rate of interest being paid to the bank on the overdraft facility is 8.25 per cent.

Figure 8.3   Pahshok plc: Balance sheet as at 31 December 1996

	£m	£m
Fixed Assets:		
Freehold property at current valuation		55.8
Plant etc at cost less accumulated depreciation		30.1
		85.9
Current Assets:		
Stocks	26.1	
Trade debtors	32.9	
	59.0	
Less: Creditors falling due within one year:		
Bank overdraft	5.6	
Trade creditors	16.9	
Proposed dividend	3.6	
Corporation tax due on 1 October 1997	5.3	
	31.4	
		27.6
Total assets less current liabilities		113.5
Less: Creditors falling due after more than on year:		
9% secured bank loan (repayable 1997/8)		42.8
		£70.7
Share capital:		
40 million shares of 50p each		20.0
Share premium		16.8
Reserves:		
Revaluation (of property) reserve		6.2
Profit and loss account		27.7
		£70.7

EXERCISE

WORKOUT

Given that under the terms of the rights issue five new shares will be issued for every 100 shares currently held, what is the amount of cash Pahshok is intending to raise?

Answer

Forty million shares are currently in issue and held by the company's shareholders (see the balance sheet in Figure 8.3). On the basis of five new shares for every 100 currently held, a further two million shares will be issued. At 425p for each new share, the total amount raised will be £8.5 million (ignoring transactions costs).

The proposal to make a rights issue resulted from the budgeted funds statement drawn up by Pahshok's corporate treasurer. The budgeted funds statement requires the following information:

★ estimates of earnings and cash generated from operations

★ estimates of interest payable and dividends to be paid in the coming year

★ estimates of the amounts to be invested in new assets.

EXERCISE

WORKOUT

Using the information that was provided above about Pahshok's current results, devise a budgeted cash flow statement for just one year ahead – for 1997.

Make whatever assumptions you need, but you may assume that the level of plant replacement and expansion that Pahshok would like to carry out in 1997 amounts to £13 million (including about £5.6 million from 'depreciation funds'). This will give some idea of the cash available for expansion – for buying additional production facilities and so on – and/or for acquisitions of other businesses (if such acquisitions were to be made for cash rather than an exchange of shares).

Answer

First of all, let us calculate some basic information about Pahshok:

Calculation of retained earnings

	£m
Profit before tax (after interest)	16.2
Taxation	5.3
Profit after taxation	10.9
Dividends	6.0
Retained earnings	£4.9

Calculation of profit before interest and taxation

	£m	
Profit after interest	16.2	
Add Interest on bank loan	3.9	(9% × £42.8 million)
Interest on bank overdraft	0.5	(8.25% × £5.6 million)
Operating profit	£20.6	

Sales are currently £187 million, so the return on sales in 1996 is 11 per cent. If it is assumed that sales are increased by 5 per cent in 1997, they will amount to £196.3 million (that is, £187 million × 1.05). As the current return on sales is 11.0 per cent, the 1997 operating profit might be expected to be £21.6 million (that is, 11.0 per cent × £196.3 million).

The budgeted funds statement, using the above information, may be set out as in Figure 8.4.

In the budgeted cash flow statement in Figure 8.4, the bank overdraft has been repaid. Should this be what the rights issue is used for – repayment of the overdraft? If so, there is only a further £1.1 million available for investment in new assets or for acquiring other companies!

Figure 8.4   Pahshok plc: Budgeted cash flow statement for 1997

	£m	£m
Operating profit		21.6
Add Depreciation (ignoring depreciation on any new assets)		5.6
Cost of servicing finance		27.2
Loan interest on long-term loans	4.4	
Dividends payable in 1997 (1996 increased by 5%)	6.3	
		(10.7)
Tax payable in 1996		(5.3)
Investing activities		
Investment in plant and equipment		(13.0)
Net cash outflow before financing		(1.8)
Financing: rights issue (ignoring the costs of the issue)	8.5	
Reduction in bank overdraft	(5.6)	
		2.9
Increase in cash balances		£1.1

The board of directors of Pahshok are aware that most of the capital raised will be used to 'restructure the balance sheet'. That is, the cash raised will be used to enable expansion by purchasing new fixed assets, but some of the cash will be used to repay borrowings, and thereby decrease the company's gearing or leverage. The board also wants to know whether or not a rights issue is the appropriate means of raising funds for the company at the present time and in its present circumstances. The next exercise asks you to consider this matter.

EXERCISE

● ● ● ● ● ● ● ● ●

Advise the Board whether it is opportune for Pahshok to make a rights issue.

WORKOUT

Answer

The answer to this exercise would be very much influenced by the state of the capital markets and economic forecasts at the time. It is not sensible to issue new shares when the markets are depressed and when the economic outlook is gloomy.

In this case you should consider whether it would be possible for Pahshok to borrow further long-term debt. The company at present is very highly geared. The *current* level of gearing of Pahshok before the rights issue is:

$$\text{Total debt divided by equity} = \frac{42.8 + 5.6}{70.7} = 68\%$$

This is a very high level of gearing or leverage and it would be unlikely that banks or other lenders would be willing to increase it. So, in this case, raising equity seems to be the only course for Pahshok at present.

Debt versus equity

In the case of a company with high financial leverage, further borrowing seems unlikely to be an acceptable source of finance. That would depend somewhat on the security that a company could offer; the value of property or other assets that could be sold to repay the loans if necessary. It is also unlikely that further loans could be obtained in a highly-geared company because the additional loans would further increase the gearing. In fact, the present holders of the company's loans or bonds would probably not allow any increase in lending. The covenants associated with the current loans of a highly-geared company would almost certainly preclude any further borrowing until their loans were repaid! Any further borrowing therefore would have to be subordinate to the current loans – that is, second in line for any distribution of funds if the company went into liquidation. Lenders of such secondary debt would demand high rates of interest, which is a major deterrent to raising more funds by way of borrowing.

An issue of shares, then, may be the only option for an already highly-geared company. A prospectus will be issued which will explain to shareholders what the funds are required for. The company may very well then use the funds raised to repay some of the debt. It may seem odd that firms could 'get away with' making a rights issue and using it to repay debt, but many companies did exactly that coming out of the recession in the years 1993–1995.

The reason why it seems odd to replace debt with equity in this way is that the *cost of equity* is higher than the *cost of debt*. This is because shareholders take the major proportion of the risk in investing in a company – much higher than that of lenders – so the shareholders require to be compensated by being offered high returns. The fact that so many companies in the 1990s replaced relatively cheaper debt with more expensive equity, can only be explained by arguing that those companies felt they were too highly geared – their financial leverage was too high – so they took the expensive step to reduce the level of debt.

The cash flow forecast based upon strategic plans will determine whether or not there appears to be a requirement to raise long-term funds. If additional finance is required, the main decision will be as to whether to issue more shares or whether to issue some debt.

There are, of course, many choices to be made within these two major categories of further finance. There are different sorts of equity – ordinary shares or preference shares or even convertible loan stock, which is loan stock that may be converted into shares at a later date. The choices under the heading of loan stock range from fixed interest term loans which have a particular repayment date to variable interest loans which have no repayment date. Loans may be secured or unsecured and they have many or few restrictive covenants. The fundamental choice, however, is between issuing new shares to shareholders or raising funds by further borrowing.

> *If additional finance is required, the main decision will be as to whether to issue more shares or whether to issue some debt.*

Whether or not debt or equity is raised at any particular point in time revolves around three issues:

★ timing, related to the current and expected level of the stock market and interest rates in particular

★ the current level of gearing or leverage

★ relative costs.

Timing

It is very important for corporate treasurers to assess correctly the current state and future movements in the finance markets. It would be poor financial management, for example, to raise a fixed interest loan for five years when interest rates were expected to fall. It would be better to wait until interest rates had fallen before the loan was arranged. It is less likely that new shares will be successfully issued on the stock market when the market is falling rather than when it is more buoyant.

A further point with regard to timing is whether or not a company already has a high amount of borrowing. If this is so – as it was in the case of Pahshok above – then the only course of action for the business is for it to issue new equity. The choice of debt is simply not a viable alternative.

Current level of gearing

Some gearing or leverage will 'gear up' or 'lever' the returns to ordinary shareholders. In good times the ordinary shareholders will receive a high return on their equity in a geared company as opposed to an all-equity company. It is true that when profits are low the shareholders in the geared company will do less well than the shareholders in the all-equity company. The following example will demonstrate this.

In Figure 8.5 we have two companies, Mink Ltd and Sable Ltd. Mink has raised all of its capital from shareholders, amounting to £600 million. Sable is a 50 per cent geared company, on the basis of debt/equity. It has £400 million of equity and £200 million of borrowing paying 10 per cent interest. As shown in Figure 8.5, when the profit before interest is £120 million the return on capital employed for both companies is 20 per cent but the return on equity for Sable is 25 per cent rather than the 20 per cent return on equity in the all-equity company Mink.

Where profits are doubled to £240 million before interest the return on equity for Sable increases to 55 per cent as opposed to 40 per cent for that of Mink. This is shown in Figure 8.6. However, if the profits fall to zero the interest on the debt in the case of Sable still has to be paid out and the

Figure 8.5   The effect of gearing (1)

	Mink Ltd All-equity £m	Sable Ltd 50% geared £m
Profit and loss information		
Profit before interest	120	120
Interest	–	20
Available for shareholders	120	100
Balance sheet information		
Equity	600	400
Borrowing (at 10%)	–	200
Return on capital employed	20%	20%
Return on equity	20%	25%

Figure 8.6   The effect of gearing (2)

	Mink Ltd All-equity £m	Sable Ltd 50% geared £m
Profit and loss information		
Profit before interest	240	240
Interest	–	20
Available for shareholders	240	220
Balance sheet information		
Equity	600	400
Borrowing (at 10%)	–	200
Return on capital employed	40%	40%
Return on equity	40%	55%

Figure 8.7   The effect of gearing (3)

	Mink Ltd All-equity £m	Sable Ltd 50% geared £m
Profit and loss information		
Profit before interest	0	0
Interest	–	20
Available for shareholders	0	(20)
Balance sheet information		
Equity	600	400
Borrowing (at 10%)	–	200
Return on capital employed	0%	0%
Return on equity	0%	negative 5%

shareholders have a negative return of 5 per cent whereas, of course, the shareholders in Mink have a zero return. This is set out in Figure 8.7.

As the graph in Figure 8.8 shows, the shareholders in Sable earn a higher return (EPS = earnings per share) than the shareholders in Mink when profits (EBIT = earnings before interest and taxation) are above £60 million. They earn a lower return when the profits are below £60 million. It may appear that the shareholders in Sable are earning a better return on average and this is so, but, on the other hand, they are taking greater financial risk. When profits fall they do worse than the shareholders in the all-equity company. The shareholders in a geared company will expect a higher return than the shareholders in an ungeared company to compensate for the additional financial risk.

Relative costs and the weighted average cost of capital

The shareholders of a company may wish the company to have a certain amount of debt, because this will gear up the returns that they receive.

Figure 8.8 EPS/EBIT chart

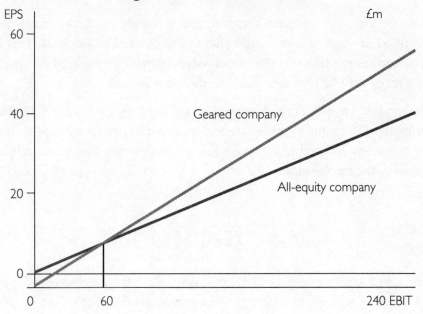

They will be aware that they are taking a greater risk, but they may be happy to accept this additional risk in the hope that they will actually receive the high return promised. From the company's point of view it is a very moot point as to whether there is any benefit from gearing at all.

The argument is that the *weighted* average cost of capital will be the same whatever the level of debt is. This can be demonstrated by using the information set out in Figure 8.9. In the higher-geared company (debt/equity is 67 per cent) the return expected by shareholders is 16 per cent and the interest paid on debt is 8 per cent. Using the weights of 90 and 60 the weighted average cost of capital calculates out at 12.8 per

Figure 8.9 Weighted average cost of capital

Company	Amount of		Cost of		Weighted average cost of capital	
	Equity	*Debt*	*Equity*	*Debt*		
	£	£	%	%		%
High geared	90	60	16.0	8.0	(90 × 0.16 + 60 × 0.08) / 150	= 12.8
Low geared	140	10	13.2	8.0	(140 × 0.132 + 10 × 0.08) / 150	= 12.8

cent. In the lower-geared company (debt/equity is 7 per cent) the weighted average cost of capital also works out at 12.8 per cent. This is upon the assumption that the shareholders in the lower-geared company only require a 13.2 per cent return on their investment.

The weighted average cost of capital is said to be the cost of capital to the company. That is the average rate it is expected to pay for its capital. It is the rate it would need to achieve on new investments. This is the subject matter of the next section.

WORKOUT

EXERCISE

Calculate the cost of equity when the company in the illustration in Figure 8.9 had £75 equity and £75 debt. You may assume that the cost of debt remains at 8 per cent.

What would you expect the cost of equity to be if the company were ungeared – that is, it had no borrowed funds?

Answer

We know that the *average* cost of capital will remain at 12.8 per cent for the company in the illustration, so we can solve for the cost of equity (CE) as follows:

$$(75 \times CE + 75 \times 0.08) / 150 = 12.8\%$$
$$\text{From which } CE = 17.6\%$$

Note: If the amount of equity equals the amount of debt, the company is very highly geared. The debt/equity ratio is 100 per cent. Consequently, the shareholders are going to look for a high rate of return to compensate for the high financial risk they are taking.

If the company is completely ungeared, that is, it has no borrowing at all, the cost of equity will equal the otherwise weighted average cost of capital – that is, in this case 12.8 per cent.

The cost of debt and equity

The *cost of debt* is taken from the knowledge a corporate treasurer may well have about current interest rates and will therefore be relatively easy to estimate with some accuracy.

The *cost of equity*, on the other hand, has been the subject of much debate. The theory suggests that what the shareholder is looking for is made up of two constituents:

★ a return equal to the return that you would receive from a basic risk-free investment

   plus

★ a return for taking risk.

The rate of return from an entirely risk-free investment is one which investors would require in a totally certain world where there was no risk of inflation or any other risk of a commercial kind. The return for risk taking is dependent upon risks which affect the financial markets generally, together with specific risk involved in investing in a particular company itself.

While that concept of the make up of the return required by equity shareholders is pretty well agreed by the academics, it has to be said that putting numbers to the concepts of the risk-free rate and the risk premium in a particular market for a particular company is much more problematical. For the sake of explanation here, we shall take it that the risk-free rate at any point in time is 6 per cent. This is akin to the rate of return that you might receive on government bonds, for example.

To add the risk element to that return, we need to estimate the risk premium for any particular company in the economy. First, we take the *average* risk premium in the market as a whole – that is, the average of all companies' risk premiums. The market risk premium we shall take to be 8 per cent. This extra return – over and above the risk-free rate – is required and expected because the returns from investments in commercial enterprises are uncertain. They can be good sometimes; they can be poor at others. So shareholders require that their expected *average* return is higher than that of the risk-free rate.

Companies which have profits that vary much as the average in the market will therefore be expected to have a return of 14 per cent. Projects which are expected to vary by rather more than the market, because they are affected by general economic forces more than the average companies in the market place will be expected to achieve, say, 4 or 5 per cent above 14 per cent. Those companies expected to have returns that are not greatly affected by general economic factors might be expected perhaps to have a return of less than 10 per cent.

Capital investment appraisal

How can we be sure of achieving an adequate return on our investment?

Assessing the need for investment in new assets

Understand net present value and internal rate of return

Payback

Taking inflation into account

The effect of inflation

A note on the estimation of cash flows

WARM-UP WORKOUT

I What do you understand by the term 'discounted cash flow'?

2 What do you understand by the term 'present value'?

3 If a revenue receipt of £1,000 is expected in one year from now, what is its present value, discounting at 10 per cent?

4 If an investment's cost is £10,000 and cash flows are expected to be £3,000 per year, what is the payback period?

5 Is a payback period of five years good or bad?

Introduction

We made the assumption in Chapter 7, that planned extensions of the business would take place, provided that the providers of finance *receive an adequate return*. How can we be sure that they will do so? The answer is that we cannot. The future is, by definition, unknown; it is uncertain. We cannot be sure that the outcome from any expansion plans will be as predicted. This creates a real dilemma for managers: whether to concentrate on what is known and continue the current business at its present level of activity or whether to take the risk of expansion; to raise new funds and invest them, riskily, in the business. If only we could be sure of how successful the new business will be, we could be sure of paying the providers of finance the return they require.

But future business, whatever it is, is inherently uncertain. Even making a decision to make no investment – to stay with the business it knows – may be taking more risk than the company which diversifies. The market for the original business may change for some unexpected reason. What managers do is seek a strategic plan of campaign, which, in their opinion, has the least risk – or is most likely to be achieved. There is a choice to be made:

1. A low risk strategy – concentrating on known markets with well tried and tested products or services. The rate of return in this case is

unlikely to be high, but will have to be high enough to meet the cost of capital

2. A higher risk strategy – new products, services, processes, technologies and innovations are taken on board (or at least some!). In these circumstances, the providers of finance will look for a higher return. They take the risk that the business *may* achieve the higher return – but also may not.

Which of these extremes – a low risk or high risk strategy – do you think your organization currently follows?

EXECUTIVE
ACTION

There are unquestionably some companies which 'seek the quieter life', and thereby attract a certain sort of investor. There are other companies, whose managements are more aggressive and who do seek out investment opportunities which they consider will provide higher than average returns. In both types of business, the level of business can go down, as well as up, although in the latter type of company, success and failure may be more extreme than in the former.

Some businesses, in some industries, *have* to take risks; albeit a calculated risk. For example, it is far from certain that the outcome of massive research and development expenditure in the pharmaceutical industry will actually result in a drug that can be used effectively for a particular illness. The risks are high, but so too are the pay-offs if you are successful.

Can you think of risky projects that have been undertaken in your own business?

EXECUTIVE
ACTION

Principles of capital investment appraisal

How can we be sure that the return required by the providers of capital is likely to be achieved from new investment? And how can we estimate how risky the investment is, so that we can give some idea to investors as to the degree of risk they are taking? Well, there are techniques used in accounting and finance that are used to appraise projects and indicate the level of risk involved. These will be described below. It has to be said, however, that a great deal of management judgement is used in deciding which investments should be undertaken. Such judgement may be based on the quantitative information collected together and presented by accountants, but capital expenditure decisions also depend upon a non-quantifiable, qualitative assessment of the risks involved.

> *It has to be said, however, that a great deal of management judgement is used in deciding which investments should be undertaken.*

EXERCISE

WORKOUT

What qualitative issues might be brought to bear in deciding to invest in the provisions of a new service, such as the direct selling of life assurance by an insurance company? Direct selling means that the company would deal with customers directly, rather than through agents or brokers. The company would therefore need an organization capable of selling to customers individually.

Answer

Assuming that the new direct selling organization would require a large number of sales people on telephones, a large capital investment would be required. That might be said to be the quantitative side of the investment plus, perhaps, the investment in the initial marketing of the new service. The outcome – the expected revenues (net receipts from policies) – might be regarded as less quantifiable, but most managers appraising such an investment would expect to see forecast sales figures in the investment appraisal figures.

The non-quantifiable and more qualitative issues would revolve around the image of the insurance company in the market now that it has changed tactics. Are members of the public willing to make decisions about their life assurance with someone over the telephone, or do they prefer to deal face-to-face with a professional adviser from a brokers? Can sufficient numbers of suitable staff be found and/or trained to meet the requirement for the necessary dealings over the telephone?

Longer-term perspectives

In Chapter 7, we saw that from the planning process there may come the realization that the business will be short of funds in the longer term. Such a business will be short of funds because its growth will require more funds than can be found from its retained earnings. The outcome of the planning decision to invest additional capital in growth can only be seen over a number of years. The growth in companies usually involves large capital investment – that is, investment in fixed assets which are going to be used over many years. The discounted cash flow techniques aid this decision-making process.

Capital investment takes place under the following circumstances:

★ where the company has some choice: investment for the expansion of the business. Buying additional assets with which or upon which to operate so that more business is done.

★ where the company has little choice: the investment really has to take place anyway:

  – where old assets that are worn out have to be replaced

  – where competitive forces are such that investment has to be made in order to keep pace with competitors.

  – where government legislation has decreed that changes be made, for example, in health and safety. An example is the massive capital investment by the water industry in the UK in order to clean up beaches, improve drinking water quality and so on.

Where the investing company has the choice, it will only undertake the investment if it provides an adequate return on capital to the providers of the capital of the business. Where the company has no choice – where the investment has to be made in order to keep the business going for one reason or another – the objective is not about obtaining a return, but carrying out the investment in the most cost effective way. Cost minimization is important in making investments which have to make a return, but for investments which have to be made, it is the only criterion.

Investment decisions are based on cash flow: the concept of present value

What happens in any of these cases, is that cash is spent, usually initially, on a capital investment in tangible fixed assets, which are used to create a product or to provide a service over the economic life of the plant or equipment. The cash generated from the income from selling the goods or services produced can then be compared with the capital cost up front. In such cases, it is the *timing* of the cash flows generated by the investment that is relevant. For example, if the initial cost of the investment in a plant was £500,000 and the project paid back £100,000 per year for seven years, this might, at first sight, appear to be a reasonable investment. You get £700K for £500K. However, it has to be remembered that the receipt of £100,000 each year is not available to the business – for investment back into the business or to pay dividends to shareholders, for example – until it is received – so there is an opportunity cost that has to be taken into account when assessing the investment.

In financial terms, we say that the £100,000 received at the end of the first year could have been invested in the business for that year, if it had been available at the beginning of the year. That £100,000 could have earned, say, a 10 per cent return over the year, so we say that the sum which could have been invested at 10 per cent to become £100,000 by the end of the year is equivalent in financial terms. Well, that sum is £90,909, because £90,909 plus a 10 per cent return would provide a cash flow of £100,000 in one year's time:

$$£90,909 + 10\% \times £90,909 = £100,000$$

In finance, we call the £90,909 the *present value* of £100,000 in one year's time. This concept is the basis of all discounted cash flow techniques.

The reason for doing this is that all the cash flows from the project can be compared when in their present value form. In the case of the example of our £500,000 investment above, if the present values, using 10 per cent as the rate of interest, of each of the £100,000 cash flows each year add up to more than £500,000, we can say that the return from this investment is more than 10 per cent. If the present values add up to less than £500,000, we can say that the return on the investment is less than 10 per cent. We shall see later that there is a technique which calculates exactly what the return on the investment is.

The present values of each £100,000 received each year are shown in Figure 9.1 and the total present value amounts to £486,841.

Figure 9.1 Present value of £100,000 per year (1)

	Cash flows £000	Discount factor* using 10%	Present value £000
Year 1	100,000	.90909	90,909
2	100,000	.82645	82,645
3	100,000	.75131	75,131
4	100,000	.68301	68,301
5	100,000	.62092	62,092
6	100,000	.56447	56,447
7	100,000	.51316	51,316
Total present value			£486,841

* the formula for the present value is $1/(1+i)^n$ where **i** is the rate of interest or return assumed to be the rate the business could have earned elsewhere; and where **n** is the number of years ahead that the cash flow is being discounted. So the discount factor for year 5 is:

$$1/(1 + .10)^5 = .62092$$

EXERCISE
• • • • • • • • •

WORKOUT

The total present value of £100,000 receivable for each of the next seven years discounting at 10 per cent is £486,841. Does this mean that it is worthwhile investing £500,000 in such an investment which returns £100,000 each year for seven years?

Answer

The present value of the £100,000 receivable for seven years, discounted at 10 per cent is less than £500,000, so this investment does not earn a 10 per cent return. The return on this investment is less than 10 per cent.

Discounted cash flow techniques

The principle of discounted cash flow is that it aims to compare projects on an equal footing – based upon the *present value* of future cash flows. In this way, all cash flows, whenever they are received or spent can be compared equally and fairly. There are two discounted cash flow techniques which use this present value approach:

★ net present value

★ internal rate of return.

Net present value

The approach of the net present value method is to find out whether the total of the present values of the future cash flows is greater than the initial capital investment. So the capital cost of an investment is deducted from the total present value of the future cash flows to see whether it is positive or negative – to calculate a *net* present value. If the *net present value* is positive then the rate of interest that has been used to find the present values has been achieved. The net present value of the example used in Figure 9.1 was negative: (£13,159) = £486,841 – £500,000, which showed that the rate of 10 per cent was not achieved.

Internal rate of return

You may intuitively be able to see that if a higher rate of interest is used then the present value of those future cash flows will be less. This is because, at a higher rate of interest, less needs to be invested now to become the cash flow later. There will be a rate of interest which, when used as the discount factor, will cause the net present value to be zero. You have to find this by trial and error – by trying various rates of interest – until you find the rate which makes the net present value nil.

EXERCISE

In the example used in Figure 9.1 – the £500,000 investment which returned £100,000 for seven years – would you guess that the internal rate of return on the investment was 5, 8, 12 or 15 per cent? [This is a pretty unfair question because, without a PC spreadsheet, we wouldn't know the answer either, but you might like to estimate the answer!]

Answer

The internal rate of return of the investment is 9.196 per cent, as shown in Figure 9.2. The total present value of the £100,000 received per year discounting at 9.196 per cent is shown to be exactly £500,000.

Figure 9.2   Present value of £100,000 per year (2)

	Cash flows £000	Discount factor* 9.196%	Present value £000
Year 1	100,000	.91578	91,578
2	100,000	.83866	83,866
3	100,000	.76803	76,803
4	100,000	.70335	70,335
5	100,000	.64412	64,412
6	100,000	.58987	58,987
7	100,000	.54019	54,019
Total present value			£500,000

We will demonstrate both the net present value and the internal rate of return techniques using the example of an investment proposal of Smartfiles plc, a manufacturer of stationery folders, files and notebooks. The company is contemplating an investment of £5 million in a new factory facility on a greenfield site. The economic life of the plant is expected to be as long as 15 years, although a major refurbishment will have to take place every five years, so the investment will be evaluated over just five years, and the saleable value of the factory building will be assumed to be £2 million at the end of the first five years and brought into the calculations at that value.

Figure 9.3 sets out the net present value calculations, using 10 per cent again as the discount factor. The cash flows are the net cash forecast to be generated by the investment in the factory over the first five years. Figure 9.3 shows that the investment has a positive net present value, discounting at 10 per cent. The return on the investment is therefore more than 10 per cent.

Figure 9.3   Smartfiles' net present value calculations

	Cash flows £000	Discount factor using 10%	Present value £000
Year 1	1,320	.9091	1,200
2	1,300	.8264	1,074
3	1,240	.7513	932
4	1,100	.6830	751
5	1,000	.6209	621
5 – saleable value of factory	2,000	.6209	1,242
Total present value			5,820
Initial investment			5,000
Net present value			+£820

Figure 9.4 shows the internal rate of return calculations, found by trial and error. First, 14 per cent is tried and net present value is found to be positive. Second, 16 per cent is used and net present value is found to be negative. Finally, 15.5 per cent is used and the net present value is zero. Thus the internal rate of return is said to be 15.5 per cent.

Figure 9.4   Smartfiles' internal rate of return calculations

	Cash flow £000	Discount factor 14%	Present value £000	Discount factor 16%	Present value £000	Discount factor 15.5%	Present value £000
Year 1	1,320	.8772	1,158	.8621	1,138	.8658	1,143
2	1,300	.7695	1,000	.7432	966	.7496	974
3	1,240	.6750	837	.6407	794	.6490	805
4	1,100	.5921	651	.5523	608	.5619	618
5	1,000	.5194	520	.4761	476	.4865	487
5 – factory	2,000	.5194	1,039	.4761	952	.4865	973
Total present value			5,205		4,934		5,000
Initial investment			5,000		5,000		5,000
Net present value			+£205		–£66		£ nil

So we have two techniques effectively under the heading of discounting: net present value and internal rate of return. Generally speaking, managers in industry tend to prefer using internal rate of return because this is the simpler of the two to communicate. It is easier to comprehend the fact that 'the rate of return on the project is 15.5 per cent' than to understand the meaning of 'the net present value of the project is positive discounting at 10 per cent'. However, the two procedures usually give the same answer although there are a number of technical reasons why financial managers actually prefer net present value.

You will need a computer spreadsheet or a programmable calculator to enable you to calculate the internal rate of return of an investment quickly. Trial and error is time consuming.

EXERCISE

WORKOUT

If you have access to a spreadsheet find the internal rate of return of the following project.

Balsam Supplies are to invest in a new automated warehouse facility, which will cost £2.3 million and which will make the following savings in company costs over the next seven years. The warehouse will have no value at the end of seven years, when it will have to be completely refurnished. The cost savings over seven years are:

	£
Year 1	600,000
2	620,000
3	590,000
4	580,000
5	550,000
6	510,000
7	470,000

Answer

The internal rate of return of the project is 16.21 per cent. At that rate the net present value of the investment is zero, as set out in Figure 9.5.

Figure 9.5 Balsam Supplies' internal rate of return calculations

	Cash flows £000	Discount factor using 16.21%	Present value £000
Year 1	600	.8605	516
2	620	.7405	459
3	590	.6372	376
4	580	.5483	318
5	550	.4718	260
6	510	.4060	207
7	470	.3494	164
Total present value			2,300
Initial investment			2,300
Net present value			nil

Net present value and internal rate of return compared

The decision rules which conclude whether or not an investment should be undertaken are each slightly different. Under the net present value technique, the objective is to see whether or not the *required rate of return* is achieved. That is, discounting at the required rate of return, is the net present value positive or negative? If the internal rate of return is calculated, the objective there is to compare it with the *required rate of return*. So, if the internal rate of return is 15 per cent, the question is whether that is more or less than the required rate of return.

You can see, no doubt, the importance of the *required rate of return* in all this. The required rate of return, as we explained in Chapter 8, is the average return required by the providers of finance to the business – that is, either lenders or shareholders. Since the shareholders accept greater risk in the business investment environment, they expect a higher rate of return. Consequently, it is the weighted average cost of the capital supplied by lenders and shareholders that is the rate of return required from an additional investment in the business. If the net present value is negative discounting at the weighted average cost of capital, or if the internal rate of return of the investment is less than the weighted average cost of capital, then the project should not be undertaken. Indeed, the shareholders will be worse off if the business does invest in such investments. By definition, taking on projects which do not cover the cost of capital will mean that the shareholders' return will be diluted.

Payback

The simplest investment appraisal technique to use is payback. Payback simply states how quickly the initial capital investment is recouped from the cash flows expected to be generated from the investment. So a £1 million investment that has expected incoming cash flows of £300,000 per year, has a payback of 3⅓ years. In this way, payback, unlike discounted cash flow methods, does not take into account the timing of the cash flows. A £1 million investment which returned £100,000 in the first year, £400,000 in years two and three and £300,000 in the fourth year, also has a payback period of 3⅓ years.

EXERCISE

WORKOUT

Calculate the payback period for each of the following investments, A and B: £11 million is to be invested in each project, but the cash flows expected from them are quite different.

Incoming cash flows

	Project A £000	Project B £000
Year 1	5,300	600
2	4,800	1,500
3	1,800	3,900
4	1,000	5,000
5	800	5,500
6	700	4,500

Answer

The payback period of project A is 2½ years and for project B it is four years.

- the cumulative cash flows of project A are £11 million after 2½ years ($£5.3m + £4.8m + ½ \times £1.8m$)

- the cumulative cash flows of project B are £11million after exactly four years.

On the basis of payback it therefore looks as if project A is a better investment. Project A gets its money back earlier than project B. This will usually mean that the internal rate of return on project A will be higher than that on project B. However, a conclusion that A is the better project is misleading because the cash returns from project B are very high in the final years. This fact is not incorporated into the payback calculation.

Cumulative cash flows and the payback periods of projects A and B can be shown graphically as in Figure 9.6.

Figure 9.6   Cumulative cash flows of projects A and B

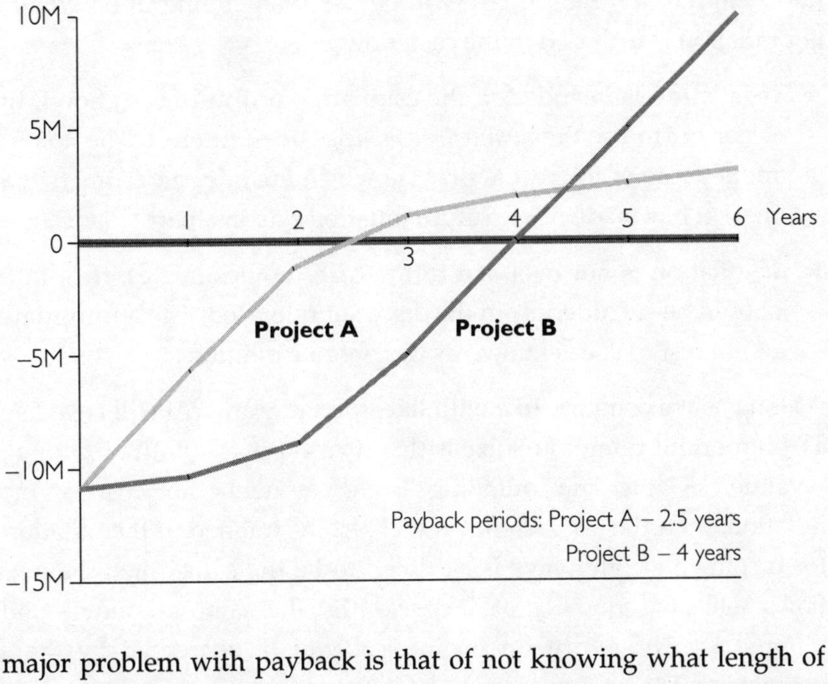

Payback periods: Project A – 2.5 years
Project B – 4 years

The major problem with payback is that of not knowing what length of payback is desirable. There is no economic calculation or guideline which suggests how long the payback period should be. It is true that in hi-tech industries such as the computer industry companies try to achieve a payback period which is no more than two to three years. For very capital intensive projects, a payback period may extend to five to seven years and that may be acceptable. There is no rationale for setting any particular length of time. For this reason payback should be given and used with care.

Inflation

When the cash flows from the investment are estimated they may include inflation, or not, as the case may be. If inflation is excluded, the cash flows will be estimated in terms of *constant* prices – that is, as if all prices and costs were to remain at the levels of today for the foreseeable future. If an estimate of inflation is included in the prices of inputs and outputs in the future, the cash flows will be in *inflated* money terms.

It is important to know whether inflation is included in the cash flows or not. A different discount rate will be used depending upon whether or not inflation is included in the cash flows:

★ If inflation is included in the estimation of future cash flows, then it is correct to use the *nominal* or *money* rate of interest. The nominal or money rate of interest is the rate which includes an estimate that the market has made of the future inflation rate in a particular economy.

★ If inflation is not included in the cash flow estimates, then inflation should be excluded from the discount rate used. The appropriate rate of interest to use is known as the *real* rate of interest.

As long as we compare like with like, the same answer will be arrived at. The important thing to realize is that if cash flows – both incoming from revenue receipts and outgoing from payments for costs – include inflation, then the *net* cash flows will also be inflated. *If* the inflation rate for income and outgoings is assumed to be the same, then the net cash flows will consequently be increased by the same amount – and the internal rate of return on the project will be increased by the same percentage. This is shown to be the case in the example in Figure 9.7.

Figure 9.7 uses the example we used earlier of an investment which was expected to return £100,000 each year for seven years from an investment of £500,000. In Figure 9.7, forecast cash flows are increased by 5 per cent inflation each year, and then discounted at 15.5 per cent. 15.5 per cent is used because the cash flows have been inflated by 5 per cent and 15.5 per cent is 5 per cent more than the 10 per cent used to discount the uninflated cash flows. Discounting the inflated cash flows at this rate gives the same answer.

Note: The rate of 15.5 per cent is used rather than 15 per cent because the calculation is cumulative (5 per cent on top of 10 per cent) rather than simply additive.

Figure 9.7 Present value of £100,000 per year inflated at 5 per cent per year

	Cash flows £000	Discount factor using 15.5%	Present value £000
Year 1	105,000	.86580	90,909
2	110,250	.74961	82,645
3	115,762	.64901	75,131
4	121,551	.56192	68,301
5	127,628	.50396	62,092
6	134,010	.45198	56,447
7	140,710	.40537	51,316
Total present value			£486,841

If we return to the earlier example of Smartfiles plc's investment of £5 million in a new factory, we can demonstrate the correct approach to dealing with inflation. The incoming cash flows from the investment were estimated to be:

	£000
Year 1	1,320
2	1,300
3	1,240
4	1,100
5	1,000
5 – sale of factory	2,000

Let us assume that these cash flows were estimated at the prices and costs at the beginning of Year 1, when the investment was made; in other words these cash flows were at constant prices. You may remember that the internal rate of return was 15.5 per cent based on these cash flows.

If we made the simplifying assumptions that the prices of the products coming out of the new Smartfiles' factory increase with inflation at the same rate as all the costs and that the expected rate of inflation will be 3 per cent, then the expected cash flows from the new investment will be:

	£000
Year 1	1,360
2	1,379
3	1,355
4	1,238
5	1,159
5 – sale of factory	2,318

The internal rate of return of the investment is now 18.96 per cent – approximately 3 per cent more than the return at constant prices.

WORKOUT

EXERCISE

● ● ● ● ● ● ● ●

Using 18.96 per cent to discount the inflated cash flows show that the net present value is zero.

Answer

Figure 9.8 shows this calculation.

Figure 9.8 Smartfiles' internal rate of return with inflated cash flows

	Cash flows £000	Discount factor using 18.96%	Present value £000
Year 1	1,360	.8406	1,143
2	1,379	.7066	975
3	1,355	.5940	805
4	1,238	.4993	618
5	1,159	.4197	486
5 – saleable value of factory	2,318	.4197	973
Total present value			5,000
Initial investment			5,000
Net present value			£ nil

Differential inflation rates

It may be that the general rate of inflation will affect all cash flows equally. Inflation of 3 per cent will increase all cash flows by 3 per cent. It is quite likely, however, that the effect of inflation on project cash flows will be uneven. There is no reason to assume that raw material prices will increase at the same rate as inflation; their prices may even be going down when there is inflation generally. Wages and salaries may increase at quite a different rate to the general rate of inflation. So it may be wise to look at the composition of the cash flows and make adjustments to each variable for the expected effect of inflation on them. Assumptions about such *differential* inflation may have quite a dramatic effect on the return expected from an investment.

Tax

• • •

We do not intend here to present the tax calculation for a particular investment but rather to make the point that tax does have an effect on the return expected from a project. This is because of the incidence of tax:

that is to say, the effect of the timing of the payment of tax on profits from an investment, and the timing of allowances that are given for capital expenditure on a project. It is very important to take tax into account in the computations because the tax payments are an important element in the cash flow estimations.

An example is given in the appendix to this chapter.

Estimating cash flows

A typical investment decision involves a large sum of cash which is paid out initially and then that is followed by a number of years when smaller cash flows are incoming, generated by the investment. It has been explained how the timing of the incoming cash flows is crucial in terms of discounted cash flow techniques, as well as payback. It has been shown how the return on an investment is compared with the return required by the providers of capital. What has not been made clear – although it is self-evident – is that the incoming cash flows used in the calculations are very much *estimates* of the future cash flows that will be forthcoming from the investment. They are forecasts of cash flows of the outcome from their investment, based upon the best estimates of managers. The cash flows may be very uncertain. The actual cash flows received in due course from the investment may be quite different from the original forecasts.

The estimate of the future cash flows may take a lot of management time to work out. Demand for the product or service to be supplied might have to be estimated, taking into account competition, competitors' prices and so on. Costs will have to be established, taking into account the methods and processes for making the product or for delivering the service. Also the costs of selling and marketing the product or service, and of administering the business, will have to be estimated over the life of the project. It is in this way, possibly after several months' work by a project team, that the cash flows expected from the investment can be suggested. The process may be summarized as follows:

★ estimate revenue stream(s) over the life of the investment

- ★ estimate the costs of producing the product or providing the service over the life of the project

- ★ estimate the selling and marketing costs involved and the costs of running that part of the business related to the investment

- ★ estimate the cost of the initial investment and its economic life.

The point being made here is that the incoming cash flows are very much estimates (the business's managers' best 'guesstimates'?) of the cash flows that will eventually flow from the investment. Consequently, the expected cash flows are usually provided as sums of money rounded to the nearest thousand pounds or US dollars. Any more precise figure would give an impression of spurious accuracy. The discounted cash flow techniques on the other hand, provide answers which give an air of great accuracy – for example, a net present value of £820,000 or an internal rate of return of 16.21 per cent (*see* Figures 9.3 and 9.5). So beware of *apparent* accuracy in this area. We just do not know the future with any degree of certainty, so we must always be uncertain as to the exact outcome of projects.

There are ways of taking account of this uncertainty in project appraisal. These methods are so important in the context of strategic finance that we dedicate a whole chapter – the next – to the inclusion of risk in the decision-making process.

Wider issues

Finally, it has to be said that it is unlikely that all the benefits and costs of undertaking a particular investment will be captured in the discounted cash flow computations. Much research has been undertaken to find out how managers actually do make investment decisions and which financial techniques they use. Many researchers have found that management judgement plays a major and important part in any capital investment decision. The most important question is always found to be: 'Does the investment feel right'? The managers taking the investment decision have to be satisfied that the new investment 'fits in' well with the company's current activities.

> *The managers taking the investment decision have to be satisfied that the new investment 'fits in' well with the company's current activities.*

Exactly how they do this is not at all clear. That is why the feeling is put down as management judgement. In Chapter 11 we show how it is possible to assess the wider benefits (or perhaps costs) of a particular investment and how those benefits might be included in the strategic investment decision.

Appendix
The impact of taxation on capital investment proposals

It is important, I would say vital, that the tax implications of an investment proposal are considered. Whatever tax regime your business is working within, the effect of tax has to be taken into account in the investment appraisal. There are two reasons for this:

1. Taxation affects the timing of the net cash flows received from an investment, and as we have seen in this chapter, the timing of cash flows is all important in the discounting process.

2. The allowances for depreciation under taxation laws or government grants towards capital expenditure should be taken into account in the net cash flows.

The effect of these matters on the cash flow calculations is such that it is quite possible that a project which appeared to have a negative net present value will have, when tax effects are taken into account, a positive net present value. You have to discount by the after-tax weighted average cost of capital (WACC) in the computations. I shall make the very much simplifying assumption here that to establish the post-tax WACC, you simply take the pre-tax WACC and 'take off tax' by multiplying by (1 – corporate taxation rate).

An example

In this chapter, an example was used of an investment of £500,000 which returned £100,000 each year for seven years. Discounting at 10 per cent, the net present value of the investment was found to be negative. Figure 9.1 showed that the present value of £100,000 per year for seven years discounting at 10 per cent was only £486,841.

If the tax rates and allowances in the UK are taken into account, the investment can be shown to have a *positive* net present value. Assume that the £500,000 investment is in some form of plant and machinery, which will be completely worn out in seven years' time. In the UK, depreciation allowances for tax purposes on such tangible fixed assets amount to 25 per cent per year – on the reducing balance, so the allowance gets smaller and smaller each year. The balance of taxable allowances left at the end of the seven years of the investment in this example have all been taken as an allowance against tax in the final year in Figure 9.9 below. In practice, such balances would be aggregated to the 'pool' of such balances held by the company making such investments, and the allowances would be spread over many more years.

The taxable income consists of the pre-tax cash flows generated by the project less the allowances for the capital investment. Such taxable income is taxed at 33 per cent in the UK and the tax is paid (or recovered) in the following year. The post-tax cash flows are discounted at the post-tax cost of capital which is taken, in this case, to be:

$$10\% \times (1 - 0.33) = 6.7\%$$

Figure 9.9 shows that, discounting at this rate, the net present value is positive.

Figure 9.9   The impact of taxation on capital investment proposals

Year	Pre-tax cash flows £	Capital allowances £	Taxable income £	Tax payable £	Post-tax cash flows £	Discount factor at 6.7%	Present value £
1	100,000	125,000	(25,000)	–	100,000	.9372	93,721
2	100,000	93,750	6,250	8,250	108,250	.8784	95,082
3	100,000	70,313	29,688	2,063	97,937	.8232	80,622
4	100,000	52,734	47,266	9,797	90,203	.7715	69,593
5	100,000	39,551	60,449	15,598	84,402	.7231	61,028
6	100,000	29,663	70,337	19,948	80,052	.6777	54,248
7	100,000	88,989	11,011	23,211	76,789	.6351	48,769
8				3,634	(3,634)	.5952	(2,163)
					Present value of cash flows		500,901
					Capital cost of investment		500,000
					Net present value		+ £901

Taking account of risk

What is risk?

We begin this chapter with a simple question about risk in investment appraisal, because it is so important to understand exactly what financial experts assume (and do not assume!) when taking risk into their calculations.

EXERCISE

WORKOUT

In your opinion or in your experience, what makes a project *risky*?

Answer

Risk, in relation to making investment, has to do with the fact that you will know what you expect or what return you want from an investment, but you will also know that you cannot be certain of achieving that actual return. Whenever any investment is evaluated, you have to remember that the assessment is based on *estimating* the future outcome – the cash flows – from the investment. The future is uncertain – all sorts of things can happen, which will affect the investment – so we cannot be at all sure about the exact return we will receive from the investment. Uncertainty about the future will make the actual return received from an investment different from the expected return. That uncertainty about the future – that not knowing what the result of an investment will be – is defined as the risk of the investment.

Risk and investments

The question as to exactly what we mean by risk relates to a fascinating area of finance, perhaps the most interesting and complex area of all. Risk in investment appraisal is the term we use to express our uncertainty about the future. The fact is that we just do not know for certain what will happen in the future, so it is difficult (impossible?) to know exactly what the actual, *definite* outcome from an investment will be.

We invest in business activity today in the expectation (the hope?) that we will receive at least an adequate return in the future. But there are so many reasons why we will not actually receive what we expected. We may receive more, rather than less, and it is important to remember that. Usually, when we think of risk, we concentrate on the negative side; we list all the things that can go wrong. But things can go better than expected and the return from an investment can be very much better than was originally thought possible.

> We invest in business activity today in the expectation (the hope?) that we will receive at least an adequate return in the future.

EXERCISE

WORKOUT

What are the changes that might happen in the future that will cause an investment to be risky? It might help to think of the events that might occur in your own organization which would affect the results of the enterprise in the coming years. You may like to consider changes that may take place within the organization separately from changes in the general economic environment, both of which may affect the performance of the company and the results from specific investments.

Answer

The reasons for the changes that might occur in the future are probably best viewed from two perspectives: from the firm level and from the general economic level.

At the firm level:

★ the product or service will be affected by unexpected changes in consumer preferences, competition, substitutes

★ the product or service will be affected by changes in technology, research and developments, new sources of raw material

★ the product or service may be affected by unexpected changes in the business environment relating to changes in environmental protection legislation, health and safety regulations, staff working conditions.

The general economic level:

★ the success of the investment will be affected by changes in general economic activity brought about by changing levels of inflation, interest rates, exchange rates

★ the investment return may well be affected by the general economic climate – the 'feel good' factor, or the lack of it – which affects the level of economic activity generally

★ the success or otherwise of a venture may be affected by political change – for example a change of government, nationalization policies, privatizations.

When we take risk into account, we are acknowledging the fact that things may not turn out as expected once we have made an investment. So many things can happen to make the outcome from the investment very much better or very much worse than originally expected. The product or service that we are providing may sell better in the market than expected. Alternatively, technical problems may arise so that the costs of making the product are unexpectedly increased, or it may take much longer to train employees to manufacture and sell the new product or service. Other factors, outside the control of the company undertaking the investment, may also affect the success or otherwise of the investment. For example, the general economy may expand more rapidly than expected or move into recession, interest rates, and therefore expected returns, may change and competition in the marketplace for the product or service may be more or less than expected.

> *When we take risk into account, we are acknowledging the fact that things may not turn out as expected once we have made an investment.*

Measuring risk

Business managers try to assess and quantify all the different outcomes in order to establish the range of good and bad news, and how that might affect the returns expected from the investment planned. In this way a whole range of expected returns may be calculated. The approach taken in financial analysis is to try to make some assessment of the degree of *variability* of return. This means that if you have an investment which is expected to have a return of 15 per cent, risk analysis would try to show by how much either side of 15 per cent the returns might be likely to vary.

Take the examples of two investment opportunities faced by a company called Protal plc: project A and project B. The internal rate of return expected from project A is 10.8 per cent and that of project B 14.0 per cent. All other things being equal, the managers of Protal, being rational investors, are expected to choose project B rather than project A because of the higher return from project B. This is because investors are assumed to want to invest where the returns are highest. If investors are told, however, that B's returns are highly variable and subject to change in market conditions, some investors may prefer project A. If it seems a safer investment, even though it has a lower return, some investors may prefer it. So the managers of Protal will have to 'know' the risk preference of their shareholders. Are they investors who like a rollercoaster experience . . . high returns sometimes, but low returns at others . . . or are they investors who prefer lower average returns which do not vary too much.

The returns on project B could be as much as 40 per cent but might be as poor as making a loss of 10 per cent each year. The variation in returns could be much less in the case of project A. Investors may estimate that the returns on project A will be no less than 2 per cent although they will not be higher than, say 18 per cent. The comparisons between the various possible returns on projects A and B are set out in Figure 10.1.

There is a *risk premium* of 3.2 per cent between the expected returns of projects A and B; that is, 14.0 per cent less 10.8 per cent. The question is: Is that risk premium adequate to compensate for the extra risk of project B? Only individual investors can make their minds up about such matters. One investor may like one investment, another may like the look of another. It is for this reason that different views are taken about investments. Furthermore, some managers and some investors would accept a higher level of risk – for a higher expected level of return – while others may not be willing to accept the risk simply for a relatively small increase in return.

Figure 10.1   Measuring risk: scenarios approach

	Expected return	Highest and lowest returns	
Project A	10.8%	{	maximum 18% minimum 2%
Project B	14.0%	{	maximum 40% minimum (10%)

EXERCISE

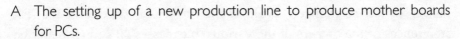

WORKOUT

Place the following list of investment proposals in order of their 'riskiness' *in your opinion*.

A   The setting up of a new production line to produce mother boards for PCs.

B   The investment by a university in distance learning materials and facilities (workbooks, computer software, warehousing and distribution) for its MBA course.

C   The scientific research into a new sun-screening lotion for holiday-makers which it is hoped will be very much more efficient than current products available.

D   The marketing and production of a sun-tan lotion which has passed health and safety tests and is ready for production.

E   The investment in a new, and much more powerful, computer database for a national opinion poll company.

Answer

It is very difficult to answer this exercise without more information. The list, in order of riskiness, would probably be as follows. You should note that this is just one opinion – the author's – and you may have quite a different order which would be arguably quite correct. The ordering is as follows:

1	C
2	D
3	E
4	B
5	A

If the expected returns from the above list of investments *and* the expected variation in return was given, it would be quite possible, from a *financial* point of view, to order the list of investments in the above exercise, much more meaningfully. It would still be left to managers to decide, on behalf of the investors they act for, which type of investment to go for: the high return, but high risk investments, or the lower return, but lower risk investments.

For example, if the information in Figure 10.2 was given about the investments outlined in the above exercise, the ordering shown in the answer would be changed. Without the further knowledge of the risk preferences of the owners of the various 'businesses', it cannot really be said which of the investments is 'better' than any other. For example, project C has the highest potential return, but the highest degree of risk.

Figure 10.2   Risk and return

		Expected return	Possible variation from expected return
A	Production line	15%	± 20%
B	Distance learning material	10%	± 6%
C	Research project	20%	± 30%
D	Marketing project	16%	± 22%
E	Database	12%	± 10%

Portfolio effects

We should also add that much would depend upon your *portfolio* of investments. It is quite possible, depending upon the correlations of returns, to take on a fairly risky investment and be better off accordingly. If you already have a portfolio which includes fairly low risk investments, the effect of combining with a high risk investment, with higher returns, will increase expected returns without a corresponding increase in the level of risk. There will be an increase in overall risk, but not so much as you might expect. In such cases, it is possible to increase the overall average return of your portfolio, without increasing the risk to any great degree. Such is the benefit of portfolio theory and analysis.

Risk in financial strategic planning

As explained above, risk in financial analysis is measured in terms of the anticipated variation that might occur in the expected return. Risk in this way may be expressed in a number of ways:

★ scenarios

★ sensitivity analysis

★ simulation

★ payback.

Let us look at each of those in turn.

Scenarios

The simplest way of looking at the risk of an investment is to look at three scenarios: the most likely outcome, the most optimistic and the most pessimistic scenarios. This will provide the kind of information shown in Figure 10.1. In projects A and B there was an expected return – the most likely return – and maximum and minimum returns. The latter returns could be obtained by estimating the very best that could be expected from the investment, on the one hand, and the very worst, on the other. Such a scenario approach provides a very simple view of the possible variation in outcomes from the investment.

Sensitivity analysis

Sensitivity analysis reviews the individual revenues and costs that have been used to determine the net cash flows from a particular investment. The objective is to find which of the inputs most affect the cash flows from the investment. Usually it has to be said, the factor which most affects the investment cash flows is the anticipated selling price of the product or service. The price you charge always appears to be a very crucial decision when making investment appraisal decisions. Another important factor in most cash flow calculations is the expected number of units of the product or service that is expected to be sold each year – particularly the number of units that it is expected will be sold in the early years of the investment.

The aim of sensitivity analysis is to look a little more closely, and in a little more detail, at the variables which cause the variability in the overall return expected from the project. Each input variable in the discounted cash flow calculation can be varied somewhat in order to find the effect of any change in the variable on the overall net present value of the project. The sort of changes that could be made would be, for example, plus or minus 5 per cent on sales volumes, selling prices, costs of raw materials, costs of labour and changes in other fixed costs. The objective is to establish which of the many variables that go into making a case for an investment are the most critical. It may be that the level of importance of the most sensitive variables can be reduced. For example, if the cost of labour was particularly important more mechanization could be considered, so that less labour was used in the project. It might be possible to aim for a higher level of labour efficiency if it were found that labour costs were crucial to the investment.

Simulation

For larger projects, for example those costing over £25 million, there are computer programs which are used to simulate a variety of outcomes, given different economic environments and other background information.

Again, the aim of the computer models is to provide a range of returns so that managers may have a measure of the degree of risk involved in the project. Simulation models can also arrange to handle cross variabilities (such as a change in unit price affecting the level of sales volume).

Payback

Quite a different approach to risk is taken by the use of the payback period as a measure of the risk of an investment.

Payback is used in the context of a risky investment by arguing that a short payback period should be sought when the expected outcomes from an investment are particularly uncertain. Payback measures the time over which the original capital investment cash is exposed. It measures how long it takes to get your money back. Consequently, if there is a situation where you have a fairly risky investment – as measured by its variability of returns – it may well be a good idea to look at the payback period to see how long it is before the original investment is recouped. This is to say therefore that a risky investment should have a fairly short payback period whereas it is acceptable for a less risky project to have a longer payback period.

Conclusion on discounted cash flow and risk appraisal

Because of the effect of discounting, it seems that the cash flows in early years are crucially important to the investment rather than those of distant years. This has encouraged the view that the use of discounted cash flow (DCF) procedures do encourage short-term rather than long-term investment decisions. While it does seem a pity that DCF techniques appear to encourage short termism, theoretically we have to accept that in an uncertain world this is most likely to be the case. Near cash flows *are* worth more than distant cash flows because of the uncertainty that exists when making investment decisions.

There is, currently, much research into such matters. Some researchers have shown that the financial markets – represented by those buying and selling shares – take more account of cash flow than was previously thought to be the case. They are not short termist in their approach to decision taking, but do take the longer view when the particular share warrants it. Managers, on the other hand, are regarded as short termist – wanting to get results fast.

The research continues. But one great step forward has been the association of the ideas of discounted cash flow with those of long-term strategy. The new approach has developed from the study of shareholder value analysis into a method for appraising strategic decisions. It is to the principles of building business value, using such techniques, that we turn in the final part of this Workout.

THE LONG HAUL

**Strategies: the holistic
approach: the big picture**

How to use Part Four

This part of the Workout considers the wider strategic issues of financial management.

You will be involved in working through examples of shareholder value analysis in order to take into account the wider issues of capital investment, whether it be in internal investment – the purchase of new assets for the business – or in external growth through the acquisition of new businesses.

The wider issues in strategic investment

The importance of management judgement

......

Uncertainty

......

Qualitative issues

......

The importance of the planning period

......

Shareholder value analysis in strategic planning

......

Estimating the cash flow drivers

......

A worked example of the use of SVA

......

Strategic value analysis

The importance of management judgement

The last few chapters have outlined the strategic finance approach to the investment decision. The main criteria for such decisions is whether or not the proposed investment will achieve the return required by the providers of finance. But it is perfectly obvious that the strategic investment decision is so complex that it is unlikely to be resolved by 'simply' calculating some numbers. It should be no surprise that if you ask managers how they make investment decisions they say that they use a good deal of judgement – as well as the financial figures. As any researcher in this area will tell you, when asked what processes and techniques they use in making decisions about investments, managers will generally place their judgement at the top of the list. The appraisal techniques – namely, payback and the more sophisticated discounting methods, internal rate of return and net present value – will be used to support, or sometimes question, the original managers' assumptions.

What we are saying here is that the managers taking a large investment decision – particularly one which affects the business strategy – will want to have a good feeling for the project. They will want to see that the investments fits in with the present organization. This is often a question of the cultural fit of the strategic investment in question. Will it be absorbed into the main business of the company or will it sit uneasily in the portfolio of businesses run within the company? Essentially does it have 'strategic fit'?

Managers really do use their judgement when deciding upon such strategic fit. Why is this? There appear to be two major factors:

1. The uncertainty surrounding the financial figures.

2. The fact that the financial analysis often does not encapsulate the whole picture.

Let us look at each of these in turn.

Uncertainty about financial figures

Chapter 10 explained why the figures used in financial appraisal are so uncertain. The exercise below asks you to summarize the factors in an investment appraisal decision which create this uncertainty.

WORKOUT

EXERCISE

What input information to the financial capital investment appraisal is uncertain?

Answer

The uncertainties may be listed as follows:

★ The cash flows are *forecast* figures – albeit based upon the management's best predictions of revenues and costs. But the future is, by definition, unknown and the forecast cash flows must be uncertain.

★ The period over which the cash flows can be expected – the economic life of the investment – is often highly uncertain.

★ The appropriate discount rate that should be used is very difficult to be precise about.

★ Often the capital cost, which is usually taken as a fairly 'concrete' sum to be spent, may be uncertain. If, for example, further R&D or technical innovation has to be undertaken, the cost of which is not yet known accurately.

The effect of our uncertainty about the future is that estimates ('guesstimates'?) are made and used in our calculations. This is perfectly acceptable, provided due care has been taken in making the estimates. But the problem of the financial approach is that, if the discounting process is used, the 'answer' achieved looks respectably accurate. For example, it is said that: 'The internal rate of return is 8.23 per cent', or whatever. This appears to be the result of a very accurate calculation but it is based on essentially *estimated* figures. We are using a very correct, and sophisticated, technique on very much estimated base numbers.

It is true to say that establishing a measure for the risk that is thought to be associated with the investment does emphasize that there is some degree of variability in expected figures, however accurate they may appear. Remember that what risk evaluation does is to provide some idea of the expected *variation* that is likely to occur. An investment with an expected return of 15 per cent, which may vary between 5 per cent to 25 per cent will be considered in finance to be less risky than a similar investment with an expected return of 15 per cent, but where the return could be zero, at worst, or 30 per cent at most.

Management judgement issues – qualitative benefits

The other reason that managers use their judgement when appraising investments is because they are able to bring all the qualitative benefits into play. The proposal may appear to be marginal from the financial point of view. It may even be negative, in that it does not seem to provide the rate of return required. But if the qualitative benefits of the scheme are included, albeit just in the minds of the managers, it may well be that the investment is proceeded with.

What accountants usually mean when they talk about 'qualitative' matters is more often than not non-quantifiable matters – or rather, benefits of the scheme which are difficult to quantify!

What accountants usually mean when they talk about 'qualitative' matters is more often than not *non-quantifiable* matters – or rather, benefits of the scheme which are difficult to quantify! It is possible to show how, what we will call the wider issues, can be evaluated and thus brought into the calculations. The methods we shall employ are drawn from shareholder value analysis which can show the effect of the project being assessed *on the whole business*. For the time being, let us consider what factors have to be qualitatively included by management.

EXERCISE

- - - - - - - - -

You have possibly been involved in a planning meeting where a project is being discussed, where the argument goes along the following lines:

'The financial appraisal indicates that this project is pretty marginal, but I feel that we should undertake this investment because . . .'.

How many reasons can you think of to undertake the project even though it gives only a marginal return?

Answer

I am sure that you can think of many examples from your own experience, but here is a selection that we have heard. Remember that this investment does meet the required rate of return set by the managers, if only just.

1   . . . we have to carry out this investment in order to keep up with competition in our market. If we do not, they will gain market share

2   . . . we need to make this investment in order to get experience of the new technologies it introduces

3   . . . we shall invest in this so that our staff are aware of the possibilities this area of investment might create

4   . . . the project fits in so well with what we do that we shall probably do better than the numbers suggest from synergies created by the investment.

Shareholder value analysis

- -

So managers add their *subjective* assessment to the figures, in order to conclude whether or not a project should go ahead. We see nothing wrong in that. Many apparently poor investments, from the financial point of view, have been pursued by companies, and they have achieved success in that way. Silly investments which appeared to have jumped over the financial hurdles have been stopped by a sensible manager saying: 'Just a minute, what about . . .'.

But this sort of approach is none the less subjective. The way around the problem is to take an indirect approach. Rather than try to quantify the qualitative benefits of the proposal, you look at the effect the investment will have on the *whole* enterprise. You try to assess either:

★ the opportunities that the new investment might create in the rest of the business, or

★ the (negative) effect of not undertaking the investment.

Shareholder value analysis enables you to do this. You can look at either the effect on the whole business of carrying out the investment, or what the business results would be if the investment were not undertaken. Shareholder value analysis (SVA) was developed to assess the value of the business using discounted cash flows rather than earnings, but it can be used for business planning. SVA uses the cash flows that are expected to be generated by the business over a number of years in the future and, in this way, alternative valuations of the business may be forecast from a variety of cash flow forecasts of the whole business. We saw in Chapter 7 how the budgeted cash flow forecast can be derived from the future plans of the business. SVA uses that base of forecast cash flows to go a step further and express the cash flows in terms of their present values in order to establish a present value of the business as a whole.

> *Silly investments which appeared to have jumped over the financial hurdles have been stopped by a sensible manager saying: 'Just a minute, what about . . .'.*

SVA is based on the assumption that the value of a business, as derived from its cash flows, is based upon a number of *drivers*. This term is used because the factors involved 'drive' the value of the business (up or down!). There are seven cash flow drivers:

★ sales growth

★ profit margin

★ taxation

★ incremental investment in fixed assets or intangibles

★ incremental investment in working capital

★ planning period

★ discount rate.

You might like to consider each of the business drivers by relating the following questions to your business or to a business with which you are familiar.

1   **Sales growth.** *What do you think the rate of sales growth will be in your business over, say, the next five to ten years? You may not expect much growth: it may be just the rate of expected inflation.*

2   **Profit margin.** *What profit margin do you make from sales revenue? Will this persist over the next five to ten years or will margins be squeezed? You may, of course, have several lines of business, each of which have their own profit margin, so you may have to 'build up' this figure in order to establish an average for the business as a whole.*

3   **Taxation.** *What is the average rate of tax that you expect to pay on your profits? This has to be rather a guess, because we do not know what government policies will be over five to ten years.*

4   **Incremental investment in fixed assets or intangibles.** *Given the rate of growth you expected in your business, what additional assets is the business going to need in order to be able to produce the extra units or to provide the extra service? As the business grows, it will almost inevitably need extra assets with which to work: new accommodation, new plant, new equipment, new computer kit, new distribution vehicles and so on. Your business may also have to acquire intangible assets – such as brands, patents and intellectual property rights (IPRs) – so that it is able to grow in the way you expect.*

5   **Incremental working capital.** *As most businesses expand there are usually more receivables (debtors) and often more inventory (stocks). There are some businesses, like retailers, who do not have any debtors, because customers pay up when the sale is made, but even retailers have more stock as the business grows. As the number of stores increases, the total amount of stock the business holds also increases. You may be in a service business which gets paid in advance, like insurance companies, computer maintenance businesses and holiday tour operators. In those cases, as the business expands, it has more and more cash – and no debtors and no stock to worry about!*

6   **Planning period.** *Over what period do you feel that you can reliably plan? For what period can you reasonably expect to be able to forecast, before your business environment radically changes, in which case estimating becomes so difficult as to render it effectively meaningless? There are some guidelines here, if you can answer the following questions in your particular industry:*

★   *How competitive is your business now? If it is fairly competitive already, it is likely that few new entrants will be attracted to it, so that the present situation may reasonably be expected to continue for some time into the future. In fact, it may become less competitive, if companies drop out of your sector.*

★   *Is it likely that there will be new entrants to your business sector? If profits in your sector are high now, this may attract new competitors. The effect of this possibility will be to reduce your growth expectations. But the question here is: when will the new competitor be able to enter your market? What is the least time before competition hots up? This will affect your answer to the length of the planning period for which you are able to forecast.*

★   *Are new products likely to undermine your current market and, again, how long will it be before they do? You will know whether or not your business is involved with products or services which are expected to be produced or delivered in a different way, or to be overtaken by substitute products or methods which will completely undermine your present business. It has to be said that this has happened, or is happening, to so many businesses in the 1990s – largely because of computer capabilities – that it is hard to think of any business that can have a planning period which is certain for more than about five years.*

7   **Cost of capital.** *Shareholder value analysis relies on the cash flows that have been estimated over the planning period being discounted at the weighted average cost of capital (WACC). Refer back to Chapter 8 for a discussion of the WACC.*

The importance of the length of the planning period

The length of the planning period is an important issue in SVA. The planning period needs to be at least five years. If you cannot plan for more than five years ahead, it is very unlikely that you can capture much of the value of a business. Five years or less allows insufficient time for the business to grow and to develop a market of its own. A period of five years or more, allows time for the business to change, for capital investment to bring back reasonable returns and for the business to establish itself in the market.

Much also depends upon what happens after the planning period. If sales are expected to continue to grow after the planning period, it may be necessary to consider extending the planning period. Most products and services – and therefore the businesses which deal in them – have a life cycle, which grows and then wanes. So it is not unusual to expect the level of business to plateau after a number of years of growth. The revenue of the business and the profits from it can be assumed to remain constant, and this is the assumption we shall use. If a substantial investment is undertaken, sales will be expected to grow for a period and thereafter to level off and profits will remain static.

The use of SVA in strategic planning

Shareholder value analysis allows managers to assess the value of the business under a number of planning scenarios over reasonable lengths of planning period, say ten to 15 years. It is true that the values of the business, calculated using the various scenarios, will be very sensitive to error in any of the assumptions about the future but at least the scenarios are *evaluated*, rather than leaving the decision entirely to management judgement. Managers will have to make up their own minds about the results from the various scenarios and whether to accept or reject the strategy, but this must be more informative than simply making the decision entirely subjectively. The various assumptions in SVA are entirely explicit, so the managers making strategic investment decisions will know which of the factors in the computations they are happy with and those with which they are not.

Making the right choice, with all the information at your disposal, still allows plenty of scope to take a successful step in the right direction – or to fall flat on your face!

Estimating the cash flow drivers

The cash flow drivers of the business value might be estimated in a number of ways:

★ based on the historical information contained in the company's accounts

★ from budgets and detailed plans of activity in the future

★ from expectations based on other businesses (either generally or in the same business sector)

★ estimates based on ideal or required drivers needed to achieve the financial objectives of the organization.

I believe the last of these methods is quite a valid approach. You work backwards. Effectively, you say that, for example, if the objective is to double the value of earnings per share over the next five years, then sales growth will have to be 15 per cent per year . . . or that margins will have to increase substantially . . . or both.

EXERCISE

Some of the information that was given about a company called Pahshok plc in a case study in Chapter 8 is reproduced in Figure 11.1 below. As far as is possible from the information provided, can you say what values might be placed on the cash flow drivers, based on the historical information provided. Remember the cash flow drivers are:

WORKOUT

- ★ sales growth

- ★ profit margin

- ★ taxation

- ★ incremental investment in fixed assets or intangibles

- ★ incremental investment in working capital

- ★ planning period

- ★ discount rate.

Figure 11.1   Historical information about Pahshok plc

Total sales for the year to 31 December 1996 were £187m.

Profits before tax (after charging loan stock interest) for the last five years are:

Year ended 31 December:	£m
1992	12.3
1993	13.6
1994	15.0
1995	16.9
1996	16.2

Answer

Sales growth. No information can be gleaned from Figure 11.1 about the rate of growth of sales, but the original case did say that 'the company had grown steadily over the last five years'. So we could argue for a growth rate of around 5–10 per cent per year (although I would not be dogmatic about that!). The growth in profit over the years from 1992 has averaged 7 per cent.

Profit margin. The profit margin, before interest and before taxation, was calculated as 11 per cent in the case study. May we assume that this will continue?

Taxation. The company pays tax at the rate of 33 per cent on its profits after tax. This works out at 25.7 per cent on the operating profit of the company, that is, on the profit before interest and taxation. This is because of the tax shield on the debt interest. We could assume that this effective tax rate will continue – as long as the financial gearing (leverage) of Pahshok stays the same. Less debt relatively will mean a higher effective tax rate.

The other four cash flow drivers. There is nothing in the information in Figure 11.1 that will guide us towards the other cash flow drivers. We need more financial information.

Shareholder value analysis calculations

We will begin by showing how SVA can be used to value a business. We shall then show how it can help in assessing strategic investments.

The calculations made to find a business value using SVA are very similar to those used to evaluate a particular investment project. In both cases, the future net cash inflows are estimated and discounted to establish a present value of the investment. The difference is that in the case of an individual investment appraisal, the present value of the cash flows is compared with the capital cost of the investment. If the *net* present value is positive, the investment meets the required rate of return. In the case of SVA, any capital cost required in the growth of the business is included in the calculations of the cash flows expected from the business. The present value of those future *net* cash flows is effectively the value of the business.

We shall continue to pursue the story of Pahshok plc. If we incorporate the values of the cash flow drivers discussed in the answer to the exercise above, together with further assumptions, we might decide upon the following values of the cash flow drivers for Pahshok, for the seven years to the year 2003:

★ sales growth – 11 per cent (a figure of less than this will not justify the current share price of 425p that was given in the original case study)

★ profit margin – 11 per cent

★ taxation – 25.7 per cent

CASE STUDY

Figure 11.2 Shareholder value analysis: Pahshok plc – 11%

Growth in sales assumed to be 11% over the next seven years

£000s	1996 £	Rate of change	1997 £	1998 £	1999 £	2000 £	2001 £	2002 £	2003 £	2003 onwards £
Sales	187,000	+11%	207,570	230,403	255,747	283,879	315,106	349,768	388,242	
Operating costs	166,400	89%	184,737	205,058	227,615	252,652	280,444	311,293	345,535	
Operating profit	20,600	11%	22,833	25,344	28,132	31,227	34,662	38,474	42,707	
Taxation		25.7%	5,868	6,513	7,230	8,025	8,908	9,888	10,976	
Operating cash flow			16,965	18,831	20,902	23,201	25,754	28,586	31,731	31,731
Depreciation	5,600	3% sales	6,227	6,912	7,672	8,516	9,453	10,493	11,647	11,647
Capital expenditure		+5%	(7,256)	(8,054)	(8,940)	(9,923)	(11,015)	(12,226)	(13,571)	(11,647)
Working capital		+5%	(1,029)	(1,142)	(1,267)	(1,407)	(1,561)	(1,733)	(1,924)	31,731
										in perpetuity
Free cash flow			14,908	16,548	18,368	20,388	22,631	25,120	27,884	264,425
Discounted at 12%	12%		13,310	13,192	13,074	12,957	12,841	12,727	12,613	119,612

Present value of cash flows	210,327
Value of long-term debt	42,800
Value of equity	167,527
	419p per share*

* Note: The value of equity is divided by 40 million shares to establish the price per share.

★ incremental investment in fixed assets or intangibles – 5 per cent of additional sales

★ incremental investment in working capital – also 5 per cent of additional sales

★ planning period – seven years

★ discount rate – 12 per cent.

With these assumptions, the total business value of Pahshok amounts to £210.3m. The calculation is set out in Figure 11.2 and an explanation of the numbers is given below. If the current level of the long-term loans is deducted from the business value, the shareholders' wealth in the company amounts to £167.5m. Dividing this by the present number of shares in issue (40m), each share can be said to be worth 419p. (The original case study stated that the present market price of Pahshok's shares was 425p).

Explanation of Figure 11.2

1. Currently sales are £187m per year. In Figure 11.2 they are expected to increase by 11 per cent per year for the seven years to 2003.

2. Operating costs are expected to remain at 89 per cent of sales for each of the next seven years.

3. Taxation amounts to 25.7 per cent of operating profit.

4. Depreciation has to be added back to profit to obtain the cash flow from operations. Depreciation has already been charged as part of the operating costs, but it is not a cash cost, rather, it is an allocation of the cash originally spent on the assets concerned. The case study in Chapter 8 provided the information that the annual depreciation amounted to £5.6m, which equalled approximately 3.0 per cent of sales. To keep things simple, this rate of depreciation has been assumed over the next seven years.

5. Expenditure on capital equipment consists of replacement for assets which have been fully depreciated and of incremental assets required because of the expansion in the business. In Figure 11.2, the capital expenditure amounts to the current year's depreciation, plus 5 per cent of the incremental sales for the year.

6. Working capital expenditure amounts to 5 per cent of the incremental sales for each year.

7. At the end of the planning period, sales are not expected to grow at all and profits are to remain static thereafter. The perpetuity value of the cash flows then expected is £264.4 million, the present value of which, in 1996, is included in the business value of Pahshok.

8. The cash flows over the next seven years and the perpetuity value are discounted by the assumed cost of capital, 12 per cent.

Strategic value analysis

After the rights issue, you may remember that Pahshok had just £1.1 million to spend on further expansion, although some expansion had been allowed for in the budget for expenditure on new fixed assets. Strategic value analysis would allow the company to see at what rate it would have to grow over the next seven years to have made the rights issue in early 1997 worthwhile. Figure 11.3 shows the value of the business and of the shares if the business were to grow by 15 per cent per year, rather than the 11 per cent estimated to be the rate of growth in Figure 11.2. Figure 11.3 has £13 million (the original budget for 1997) plus the additional £1.1 million invested in fixed assets in 1997 (that is, £14.1 million).

You can see from Figure 11.3, if all the other assumptions remain the same, that the value of the business is increased from £210.3 million to £247.8 million – an increase of about 18 per cent in the value – but, of course, there are now more shares in issue after the rights issue. The value per share would rise, however, as shown in Figure 11.3, from 419p per share to 488p per share. If this were to happen, the rights issue will have been considered a success.

The question is: Do the directors of Pahshok believe that the sales will increase by 15 per cent per year for seven years rather than the original 11 per cent? Even if they do have such belief in the company, can they convey that optimism to the market? The time to make such claims is at the time of the rights issue, when the company will have the attention of the financial press.

Figure 11.3 Shareholder value analysis: Pahshok plc – 15% growth

Growth in sales assumed to be 15% over the next seven years

£000s	1996 £	Rate of change	1997 £	1998 £	1999 £	2000 £	2001 £	2002 £	2003 £	2003 onwards
Sales	187,000	+15%	215,050	247,308	284,404	327,064	376,124	432,542	497,424	
Operating costs	170,800	89%	191,395	220,104	253,119	291,087	334,750	384,963	442,707	
Operating profit	16,200	11%	23,656	27,204	31,284	35,977	41,374	47,580	54,717	
Taxation		25.7%	6,079	6,991	8,040	9,246	10,633	12,228	14,062	
Operating cash flow			17,576	20,212	23,244	26,731	30,741	35,352	40,654	40,654
Depreciation	5,600	3% sales	6,452	7,419	8,532	9,812	11,284	12,976	14,923	14,923
Capital expenditure		+5%	(14,100)	(9,032)	(10,387)	(11,945)	(13,737)	(15,797)	(18,167)	(14,923)
Working capital		+5%	(1,403)	(1,613)	(1,855)	(2,133)	(2,453)	(2,821)	(3,244)	40,654 in perpetuity
Free cash flow			8,525	16,987	19,535	22,465	25,835	29,710	34,166	338,787
Discounted at 12%	12%		7,612	13,542	13,904	14,277	14,659	15,052	15,455	153,250

Present value of cash flows	247,751
Value of long-term debt	42,800
Value of equity	204,951

488p per share*

*Note: The value of equity is divided by 42 million shares, after the rights issue, to calculate the price per share.

From a strategy point of view the board of Pahshok will know what they have to achieve. We have considered only one driver, sales growth. But the directors will know that with such an injection of new capital into the company a rate of growth of less than 11 per cent will not do. For example, if growth amounts to 13 per cent per year for the seven years, the present value of Pahshok's share would be 458p. The Board could carry out such sensitivity analysis to find out what the minimum growth rate needs to be to make it worthwhile going ahead with the rights issue.

The Board might feel that the risks in the investments to be undertaken after the rights issue are higher than those of the present business. This could raise the cost of capital to Pahshok. Shareholders might expect a higher return for the higher risk. If the cost of capital was 13 per cent rather than 12 per cent, the present value per share assuming 15 per cent growth would only be 434p – not much above the current share price.

The whole picture

Remember that this process takes into account the potential growth of the whole of Pahshok, not only the extra sales generated from the new investment in the fixed assets. This is the whole point about shareholder value analysis. It allows you to bring into account the effect of expansion upon the whole business. For example, sales in a new market or sales of a new product may well encourage growth in the business's other products or services. It may create a new air of growth and development in the whole company, so that employees feel good and a new spirit in the company will create new ideas, an expansion of the business and the expected, required growth rate of the whole business is easily achieved.

SVA measures this success by showing the effect of sales growth (or the effect of changes in the other variables) directly upon the value of the business. Alternatively, managers can see what they have to achieve if an investment is proposed, but more particularly they can readily take into account the effect of the investment on the whole business. They can evaluate the wider benefits coming from the investment.

Organic growth or growth by acquisition?

WARM-UP WORKOUT

1 Do you know the difference between organic growth and growth by acquisition?

2 Do you know where the cash comes from for organic growth or growth by acquisition?

3 What makes an acquisition successful from a financial point of view?

4 Do you know why acquisitions might fail? What is meant by failure, in this context?

5 Do you know how acquisitions are financed, if not by cash?

How should we grow?

One of the major strategic financial decisions an enterprise has to make is whether it should grow organically or by acquisition. It is for this reason that we end this Workout with this topic. Organic growth means developing the firm's own activities, probably by breaking new ground, which may be hard going. Growth by acquisition means increasing the level of business by acquiring other businesses which are already active – arguably an easier route because the market for the products or services has already been established.

Companies grow as a result of investment using their retained earnings. Retained earnings are the profits left after paying tax and paying out interest to lenders and dividends to shareholders. Primarily, retained earnings ploughed back are used to replace assets which have depreciated, and to increase working capital if sales have been increasing. Any further funds available will be used either to make new direct investment in fixed assets or to acquire other businesses. Figure 12.1 summarizes the use of retained earnings. Of course, as we saw in Chapter 8, further funds may be raised from the company shareholders or its lenders in order to fund such growth if the retained earnings are insufficient for the level of growth anticipated.

Figure 12.1   The use made of retained earnings

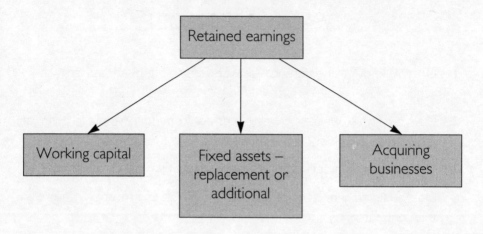

Where growth takes place

Any growth which takes place will often be in markets with which the business is already familiar. Alternatively, it may be in new markets – ones which are new to the managers of the business, where they will have to build up experience. Furthermore, new products or services may be developed and these can be marketed in current markets or in the new markets. Figure 12.2 shows the matrix of the alternatives.

Figure 12.2   Growth in markets or in products or services

	Present market	New market(s)
Current products/services	Current situation	Market development
New products/services	Product development	Diversification

The growth of current products or services within current markets is usually funded from retained earnings and further direct investment in new fixed assets will be most likely. It is possible, even here though, that market share can more readily be 'won' by acquiring competitors in the current marketplace. Often, however, growth can only take place if the company moves into related markets or diversifies entirely. In such cases it may be possible to diversify by direct investment but almost certainly it will be quicker if a business that is already a going concern is acquired.

The question is: How does a company decide whether to invest directly or by acquisition? It seems the answer to this depends upon time and, possibly, access to markets. If a business which is a going concern is acquired, it will already have been through the process of bringing its products or services to the marketplace. That takes time to do and that time is avoided if a business is acquired. If the same resources are established by setting up in a particular business sector from scratch, that takes time. A current enterprise already in business which may be a target for takeover will have:

★ an established market share

★ an established management team (with skills, knowledge of market, knowledge of customers' needs)

★ established resources (assets already up and running)

★ proven technology

★ a contented workforce (possibly)

★ satisfied customers (possibly)

★ established relations with suppliers.

The financial perspective

From the financial point of view the decision boils down to 'just another financial decision about investment'. If there is to be direct investment in new fixed assets, the appraisal can be in the form outlined in Chapter 9 – using capital investment appraisal techniques. If the investment is by acquisition, the acquirer expects cash flows to be generated from the company acquired, just like those expected from a direct investment in assets in the business. Those cash flows are then discounted to establish their expected total present value. Cash or shares are offered to the target company's shareholders and this is equivalent to the capital cost of a direct investment in fixed assets. The invested capital of the acquiring company is compared with the forecast present value of future cash flows to see whether or not there is a positive net present value from the investment.

The major difference between a takeover and a direct investment within the company is that there is often much more emotion in the takeover situation. It is not simply a question of the 'cold' financial analysis of the cash flows. There are other matters to take into account:

★ strategic fit

★ the perception of an aggressive bidder in the marketplace

★ relations with the target company's management

★ effect on staff morale

★ synergies.

WORKOUT

EXERCISE

In each of the following cases say whether you think the acquisition fits the acquirers' strategy.

1 An international liquid pump engine manufacturer is considering an expansion into the gas pipeline pump engine business.

2 A chocolate manufacturer is considering buying a large soft drinks company.

3 An international diversified industrial company (a 'conglomerate') is considering the purchase of a flour milling and food processing business.

4 A large computer software manufacturer is thinking of acquiring a group of companies which issues credit cards and offers other financial services.

Answer

1 There may appear to be a fit here, but the technologies may be very different – and the customers too. So the company may be breaking into an entirely new market with an entirely new product.

2 There may not appear to be much synergy, but both chocolate and soft drinks are sold through the same outlets (in many cases) and they are both very much consumer products. And, of course, we have the British example of Cadbury Schweppes which has been a successful merged company for over 25 years and combines these two products.

3 Arguably, any acquisition will fit into a diversified industrial. In this case we have the example of the British diversified group, Tomkins, which successfully took over the flour miller and food producer, RHM, in the early 1990s.

4 This seems an odd combination on the face of it, but there may be strategic fit if, for example, the combination is in the form of vertical integration. The software manufacturer will currently produce software for the financial institution and sees benefits – securing its market, better profits – in acquiring a foothold in that area of business.

Valuation and the acquirer

The calculation of the value of an acquisition target is an art rather than a science. Just like any other investment, the purchase of another company involves making forecasts about the future, which can never be certain. It might be possible to establish the financial strength of the target – on the basis of its published financial accounts – but to know how the company is going to perform in the future may be very difficult indeed. It might be different if the bid is accepted by the target company's management in the first instance. In an undefended bid the management team of the acquiring company will often have access to much more information. For example, the acquirer may well have access to the target company's forward budgets.

Whatever the case, the acquiring company should be very careful not to pay too much for the target. If too much is paid for the target company, the shareholders' wealth in the acquiring company will be diminished. If the cash flows expected to be generated from the acquisition do not stand up against the amount paid, the takeover will create a negative net present value and a reduction in the acquiring company's value as a whole.

> *It might be possible to establish the financial strength of the target – on the basis of its published financial accounts – but to know how the company is going to perform in the future may be very difficult indeed.*

The problem is that the right price to pay for another company is so difficult to assess. There is not only the question as to whether the cash flows expected from the acquired company will in fact be achieved but there are the ramifications of the acquisition on the business of the acquiring company to consider too.

An acquirer will usually depend upon synergies that result from the takeover. The acquiring company in the event of a merger or large takeover will almost certainly expect to gain from the acquisition as well.

WORKOUT

EXERCISE

What benefits can you think of that there might be for the *acquiring* company following an acquisition?

Answer

There may be many benefits accruing to the acquirer. The following list includes those that we have come across:

★ hope to gain access to markets that they were currently not in

★ hope to have access to staff skills, for example in research and development, that they do not currently hold

★ they may hope to have access to production facilities of a higher technical nature than they currently hold

★ they may expect to have access to sales channels that are new to them

★ they may expect to achieve economies of scale that are currently not available to them.

The wider issues and management judgement

As with all investments – as we showed in Chapter 11 – there are wider issues which are difficult to quantify but are just as much part of the management decision process. So it is in the case of takeovers. A particular acquisition may just seem to 'fit'. So management judgement in takeovers plays just as important a role as it does in the case of any other strategic decision. As we saw in Chapter 11, shareholder value analysis can be used to assess the value of the business to be acquired, and it can be used to try to evaluate the intangible benefits of the acquisition.

The first thing for the acquirer to do is to compute a value which we may call the 'acquirer's first value'. The acquirer has to make estimates of the drivers of cash flow. So the acquirer estimates future sales growth, profit margins, tax rates, investment in fixed assets and working capital and so on. If the target company is a quoted company, the acquirer's first value can be compared with the target's market value:

> **Market value   =   market capitalization**
> **=   present share price × number of shares in issue**

If the company is not quoted on a stock exchange, the acquirer will have to take a view as to whether the acquirer's first value looks reasonable in terms of being successful for a takeover at that value.

If there is a positive gap between the acquirer's first value and the market value – the acquirer's value is higher than the market price – a bid could be made at the market price, or perhaps a little higher. If there is a negative gap between the two values – the acquirer's value is lower than the market price – it may seem that the bid should not proceed. However, there are a number of other considerations.

1. The acquiring company may feel that it can make changes within the target once taken over, to improve sales, margins, investment and so on.

2. The acquirer may see opportunities to rationalize the businesses in the target company. It could sell off some parts of the business, on the one hand, or expand through acquiring other businesses, on the other.

3. There may be benefits to the acquirer's present business resulting from the acquisition; for example, the acquisition may open up markets that were not apparently available to the acquirer.

4. There may be savings that can be made because duplicate facilities will not be required; for example, corporate costs should be saved.

Ideally any first valuation by the acquirer should be calculated by carrying out a valuation of each of the individual business units, then combining them. In a contested bid, this may not be possible. It will just not be possible to obtain sufficient detail of business units from outside the group. It is for this reason alone that the acquirer's first value may be different from the market value of the company. The acquirer, on the one hand, or the market, on the other, could be making quite different assumptions about the future of the individual parts of the business. If it is possible to obtain the information about individual business units, then the individual cash flows forecast for each business should be estimated and discounted in order to establish a value for each of them. It may be necessary to use different discount rates for the various parts of the business depending upon the different types of risk faced by the various businesses.

The success of takeovers

The probability is high that the results of the takeover will not be a financial success. The chance that shareholder wealth can be enhanced by acquisition is low. Studies have shown that it is only when relatively small companies are acquired, which are in the same line of business, that the level of success following takeovers improves. When a target is large, but in an unrelated line of business, the success rate is very low. So the conclusion is that diversification is not a good thing, not a good motive for mergers. Mergers and takeovers are only relatively successful when there are combinations of companies in more or less the same industrial sector.

> Studies have shown that it is only when relatively small companies are acquired, which are in the same line of business, that the level of success following takeovers improves.

Why do so many acquisitions not increase the value of the acquiring company? The takeover may be unsuccessful simply because it is not managed well. For example, the cultures of two managements and staff may be difficult to combine. Furthermore, the outcome of the acquisition may be affected by bad luck: the economy may take a turn for the worse, the acquired company's products may go out of fashion or may be overtaken by new technology.

EXERCISE

What other reasons can you think of that might cause a takeover not to be financially successful?

Answer

Whatever the benefits that were expected to be forthcoming from an acquisition, the likelihood is that there was a degree of over-optimism in the appraisal. Consequently, it may be found that optimistic assessments were made of:

★ the expected increase in market share that would be achieved from the acquisition

★ the expected cost savings that it would be possible to make

★ the synergies that would be achievable.

A significant reason for the lack of success in takeovers is that acquirers pay too much. Several studies have shown that the premium paid over a current share price by a takeover bidder will be as much as 20 to 40 per cent. This may be just too much to pay for a company. The extra market potential and cost savings that can be made just cannot be seen to add that sort of value to a company. Consequently, it is extremely difficult to justify the price paid from subsequent profitability of the company acquired.

Finally, there may be real problems in integrating the business of the acquired company with that of the bidder. Not only are there likely to be difficulties with the practical issues of combining markets and production methods, but there may well be very different management styles to integrate. The culture of two companies may be very different and all the good works that a management in the acquired company may have achieved in the past, may be lost if they are at crossed swords with the management team of the acquiring company.

The fact is, as the research shows, that many acquisitions do not perform as well as the acquirers originally anticipate. What, then, can the acquirer do to make sure that the acquisition succeeds?

★ Identify the likely problem areas.

★ Have set strategic goals (for the acquired company and the group as a whole).

★ Have a clear timetable of activities that need to be carried out.

Financing acquisitions

The form of financing offered to a target is important both in determining the reactions of its shareholders to a bid and in its impact on the future of the new group that results from the takeover. Different forms of finance carry with them differing risks and costs to the acquirer. All can have an effect on the future business activities of the bidder.

Different forms of finance also have different attractions to different companies in different circumstances. Finding the correct structure to suit the needs and position of the company is an important element of the acquisition process. The reason for this is that there are a number of ways of paying for an acquisition:

★ cash – the most common form

★ cash combining debt

★ vendor placing – new shares 'placed' with institutions (rather than sold to all shareholders by way of a rights issue) to raise cash for the acquisition

★ earn outs – the acquirer agrees to pay for the takeover as a proportion of the profits over a period of years rather than a cash amount at the outset

★ shares in exchange for shares

★ loan stock (or debentures) for shares.

The effects of an acquisition on the financial profile of the new group

The various types of payment – whether by cash, by debt, or by offering shares – will have an impact not only in terms of whether it is accepted or not by the target, but also upon the financial structure of the acquiring group. In the short term it is important that the arrangement is suitable to both the acquirer and the target. Longer-term considerations need to be borne in mind to reflect the growth of the business. A number of issues come to mind:

★ the market values of both the acquirer and the target company shares during the takeover process

★ the effect of the takeover on the earnings per share and the PE ratio of the acquiring company

★ the effect of the acquisition on the gearing of the acquiring company

★ the effect of the acquisition upon the risk profile of the new group.

There is no such thing as a perfect bid structure. A variety of often conflicting factors need to be borne in mind. A successful bid will persuade the target shareholders to accept and fit into the acquirer's financial structure without threatening liquidity or arousing the hostility of the investors. Quite how successful the acquisition is may well depend upon the process to integrate the company taken over with the remainder of the group.

EXERCISE

• • • • • • • • •

As a final exercise, can you list a number of considerations for a successful acquisition and its integration into the larger group?

Answer

There are obviously many reasons for success (although there may be as many reasons for failure), but thinking positively, the reasons for success include:

★ the new company fits in well with the acquirer's business

★ the expected synergies are forthcoming

★ the new company's management are absorbed successfully without too much trauma (but the acquired company's management are given enough autonomy to carry on managing their own affairs)

★ staff across the group are motivated by the energy created from absorbing the new company

★ there is, at the end of it all, a common strategy for the group.

A final comment

This brings us to the end of the Workout. I feel bound to say that many of the exercises you have worked through need to be applied and re-applied in your business. The Workout has been just like taking a keep-fit course at the gym. First you do exercises to get yourself in trim, to get physically fit. Then, as any instructor at the gym will tell you, what is just as important is that, once fit, you continue the training in order to remain in good shape. So, too, with financial strategy. Once the business is financially sound, it takes a continuous effort to keep it that way. Business managers cannot let things slide; if they do, it takes a good deal of effort to get the business into shape again. And remember, if you don't keep the business fit, there may be others in the wings who will be willing to undertake that task for you!

Index